My gardens sweet, enclosed with walles strong,
Embanked with benches to sytt and take my rest:
The knotts so enknotted, it cannot be exprest,
With arbors and ayles so pleasaunt and so dulce.

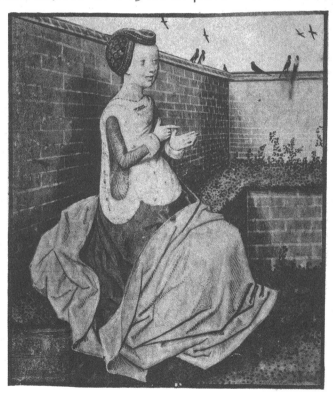

A GARDEN
IN VENICE

THE CORTILE.

A GARDEN IN VENICE

BY F. EDEN

FRANCES LINCOLN LIMITED
LONDON NW5   MMIII

A Garden in Venice
Frances Lincoln Ltd, 4 Torriano Mews,
Torriano Avenue, London NW4 2RZ
www.franceslincoln.com

Postface by Marie-Thérèse Weal
© Frances Lincoln Ltd 2003

This book has been published at the suggestion of
Marie-Thérèse Weal, who would like to thank
David Kendall for all his diligent and precious help.

British Library Cataloguing-in-Publication Data
A catalogue record for this book is available from
the British Library

First published in 1903 by *Country Life*,
Tavistock Street, London.

First Frances Lincoln edition 2003.

ISBN 0 7112 2205 3

Printed and bound in Italy by Conti

9 8 7 6 5 4 3 2 1

The Lord God planted a garden
In the first white days of the world ;
And set there an angel warden,
In garments of light enfurled.

So near to the peace of Heaven,
That the hawk might nest with the wren ;
For there in the cool of the even,
God walked with the first of men.

And I dream that these garden closes,
With their shade and their sun-flecked sod,
And their lilies and bowers of roses,
Were laid by the hand of God.

The kiss of the sun for pardon,
The song of the birds for mirth—
One is nearer God's heart in a garden
Than anywhere else on earth.

DOROTHY GURNEY.

CHAPTER I

HE garden in Venice whose story I would tell was once a bank of mud. Unconscious of its sweet destiny for thousands of years it lay inert in the lap of Adriatic waters. The south wind blew then as it blows now across the Libian Desert, and hurried on to quench its thirst in the Mediterranean Sea. Across

that sea and up the Adriatic it carried the moisture by wind and sun evaporated north to the chain of Alps that bound the Veneto. There condensing in the cooler atmosphere, the vapour turned to rain—the rain which once washed up the garden and now fertilises it. This rain, where nothing in this world stands still, had no sooner done its genial work on mountain side and plain than it hastened to the seas from whence it came. In its reasoned, if reckless, haste it cut canals through the sleeping mud, throwing up the displaced ooze on either hand to dry and harden. On such soft stuff the islands in time were formed where now stand Venice and the Giudecca.

This law or accident of Nature that in the first ages made the islands now orders the weather of our modern days. There are but four winds on the Giudecca where the garden stands, though the head of the Observatory may write the signs of more ; but then, the Venetians say, he must show something for his *salario*. First, the Scirocco, that south wind from Africa that becomes south-east with the trend of the Adriatic ;

2

then its opponent and conqueror, the north-east wind the rude Bora, that, acknowledging no bounds nor master, keeps to the road it has beaten for itself, regardless of the coast lines it severely punishes. Of less importance and weaker mind, Levante, the east wind that follows the course of the sun; and Garbin, south-west, that leaves the weather as it finds it, in Giudecca language, "*Lascia quel che trova.*"

It is Scirocco and the Bora that have made the Venice islets and that now rule them. The first brings the moisture, the last turns that moisture into rain. And so we have the apparent contradiction, that has made many a tourist distrust his aneroid, of a rising glass with a falling rain.

The contest between our master winds threw up in past ages a bank here and there, awash with the surface of the tide, to warm into life under the kiss of the summer sun. On this·the wind and wave drove and left the soil, the sand, the vegetable matter, borne by the salt tide and the fresh torrents from mainland. Here and there fell a seed or root, torn from in or under water, soon to grow into the many plants we call seaweed ; a salt forest to give food and shelter to millions of animalculæ that gave food and sport to thousands of small fishes.

As these seaweeds ripened, dried, and sank, their remains gave root-hold and sustenance to others, fending off the canal waters and adding each its mite to the ever rising bank ; until, in countless generations of plant life, the plants, little knowing that they were beneficial workers, prepared the way for other plants and wrought their own extinction.

Then the fresh torrents from mainland gave their aid. Seeds from the shore, roots from dry earth, were borne seawards on the flood and left stranded. Some, when life was still in them, to take root and grow, and so to thicken, strengthen, and protect the bank that saved them. Their work done, to give place, as happily seems the rule on earth, and must be in the universe, for something better.

So the dry land that was to be our garden was slowly made, and surely fitted for life on a higher

4

scale. Man came now to carry on the work of nature. Escaping from the mainland with life, happy if his skin were whole, he built himself a shelter of reeds, then a cabin of wood, then a cot of burnt earth or brick. Round the cottage the earth grew solid. There is no waste absolute, or loss entire, in God's law. What is rubbish at one time or place serves a wholesome purpose at another, and as man built his better building the old discarded matter took another form and certainly a fairer.

"There is some soul of goodness in things evil, would man observingly distil it out." He does and rightly does, poor fellow, wittingly or of pure instinct, get from most things as much of good as from them may be got, and so the mud, and dirt, and dust heap, become dry land, was dug and planted, and its crops coming to useful life helped sustain it. The necessary attained, his stomach filled, his eye sought to feed its soul with form and colour. Thus in time grain and roots gave some place to flowers and fruit, till with added charm and beauty, there blossomed

5

out a garden. But before this happy climax ages passed and much work was needed.

Fortunately to our gain, if to others' loss, society in the *cinque cento* was not perfect. Men and women were rarely safe out of patrician houses, or away from under that sign of peace, the Church. So Monasteries set up this sign on every islet in the Lagoon of Venice, and one on the Giudecca fenced in with a thick wall from depredation of man or encroachment of the tide, the plot of ground of which I write.

To the monks we owe the present gardener's cottage, and the sign of the Cross that decorates, and, let's hope, blesses it.

Then the monk gave way to the patrician who built the so-called Palazzina for the pleasure of himself and friends, that, conscious maybe of its worldly purpose, turns its shoulder to the Cottage Cross.

Perhaps the life of the one was as good as the life of the other, in any case they were both useful even if they did not mean or know it; for they dug and planted, or made dig and plant, and we

6

THE GARDENER'S COTTAGE.

profit by their labour. A labour from which was born the beauty that is our gain. If the man who makes two blades of grass grow where one grew before deserves well of his fellows, surely he who turns plainness into beauty should be put upon a pedestal for worship, and, better still, for imitation.

CHAPTER II

ENICE is a delightful place for man, sick or well. It was in the less happy state that I drifted to and took root in it more than a score of years ago. One floated in a gondola without the pain or stress that were from me exacted by bath-chair or carriage.

A GARDEN IN VENICE

No noise, no flies, no dust. An air so gentle that it could scarce be called a breeze. A sun that warms and rarely burns : a light, veiled white and soft, that lets one read without glare-made fatigue ; a climate which asks no man to do anything, and is answered affirmatively by all. So we, too, should have been content not to do.

The more so that in Venice there is no monotony. Of all places on earth it is the most variable in its moods. The changes in its colour are as great from day to day, and sometimes from hour to hour, as in more northern climes from month to month, or even from season to season. This variableness, the despair of her studious student, is the joy of her loitering lover. The painter finds a lovely subject, indeed they are all around him, and goes from his first day's work, and perhaps his second, content that he has caught the tone that charmed him. Even as he says so a change comes on that makes him doubtful of that work. The golden light has become silver, the cool blue shadows are swimming in a *cinque cento*

10

richness. He must alter his whole scheme of colour or go home. The next day it may be worse, and he may wait for weeks for the effect that he had not quite time to render. Thus it is that finished studio-painted pictures of Venice so rarely tell of Venice to the man who knows it, whilst the quick sketches made by the artist who can see, and is possessed of the hand that can render, faithful to his eye and taste, are so very lovely.

To the idle man this change of mood and colour is, or should be, perfection. He should never tire, and rarely does so, of his fickle mistress. He is floating to-day where he floated yesterday. The lagoon, the island, the buildings are all the same, but how different ! The Euganean Hills, or perhaps the Alps, that spoke to him of Shelley, or of snow, the distant line of *terra-firma* that held, as in a fine cut frame, the steely lagoon waters, are now hidden in a mist of light. The Ducal Palace, the Salute's dome, that yesterday appeared clear and earthly, the grand Campanile of San Marco—alas that it has fallen a victim to its own weight and Time's corrosion—the scarcely less beautiful Campanile of San Giorgio, whose clean outlines stood out so sharply in the atmosphere of vivid blue, to-day all swim ethereal in a golden haze. 'Tis all there, but a dream rather than a reality, a spirit picture more than a motive for a sketch.

Alas ! to the most faithful come moments of aberration. Man is never wholly contented. Adam and Eve, I fancy, were perfectly sick of Paradise before they sinned to leave it ; and I, a petty descendant with inherited longing for action and of change when I could do nothing, got tired day after day of doing it. One's eyes got satiated with the very beauty of palace and church, of sky and of sea, and my nerves, ajar with the perfection of repose, broke out one afternoon more lovely than its fellows, and said, " I'm sick of all this water. I'm tired of pink and grey, of blue and of red. I thirst for dry land and green trees and shrubs, and flowers ; a garden." I was answered, " A garden." You know we have asked for one everywhere ; there's no such thing in Venice. If there were, what good. Does not the proverb speak of " *Venezia, tomba dei fiori* " ?

We were floating on the Giudecca canal and the proverb, that I had heard before, was too much for my sick temper, and it cried out, " *Via via, a terra*, Eugenio. Get out and find me a garden." And Eugenio answered, " *Si Monsignore.*"

CHAPTER III

THE Venetian gondolier of the old, the true, the delightful type, says what he thinks you would like him to say. If you are going a picnic, or you are making hay, he assures you that the wind is from *terra-firma*, and the sun will shine all day. If your flowers need rain, or

15

your grass is burnt, he swears in the teeth of the north wind that it is scirocco, and the rain will fall when the tide shall run to sea. If you ask him to do what is easy, he says, "*Sì, Signor*," and will do it if it suits him so to do. If you ask him an impossibility, or what he thinks will not *tornare a conto*, his "*Sì, Monsignore*," gives you a grade or two of rank as compensation for not doing it, and an assurance to the knowing that it will not be done.

But I was flushed with my feeble effort of self-assertion and put him on shore. One had scarce time to cool when I heard Federico from the *poppe* behind, "See, Signor, ecco Eugenio, he has found it." Truly there was Eugenio on the bridge of the Rio della Croce directing us to turn out of the Giudecca canal and follow him up the Rio. We did so, rowing up the small canal to a gate near by that once had had pretensions.

As it stood, Eugenio, with an air declaring that there was no whim of his Paron's, however monstrous, that Eugenio d'Este was not equal to; and at his side an enormous blue plush waistcoat,

16

ENTRATA PER MARE E PER TERRA.

radiant with green glass buttons. Inside the waistcoat, a mere accident thereof, was Pietro "Ortolano." Pietro looked doubtful, till at that open sesame, *Una buona lira*, the waistcoat pocket gaped, and Pietro changed his chill frown of doubt for a servile grin of welcome.

We landed in a scene that neglect would have made repellant out of Italy. There stood the Cottage of the Monk, the Palazzina of the Patrician. In front of the Palazzina was a small cortile, and in the centre was a well, both fenced in with an ugly iron rail. In front again, across a broad deep-trodden path, was a tiny square of garden, closed in with an unshapely hedge of thuya and euonymus. Four grand cypresses growing in the angles within the hedge, straight and strong, seemed and seem, to point to heaven. Statues and stone vases, deftly carved with fruit and flowers, had stood on pilasters in front of the Palazzina, but these were mostly on the ground. Two arbours, one of yellow jessamine, one of honeysuckle, leant on the round stone tables they once had shaded. There were flower-beds too laid out in islands of various shapes, with paths like small canals serpentining among them. These beds still held aged plants of sweetbrier, cabbage, and moss roses, with iris and white lilies, their bulbs struggling for existence half out of the ground, seeking in the air the nourishment an exhausted soil could no longer give them.

Outside the hedge, vines were planted in straight and crossing lines, and within the squares made by the vine-pergolas grew, seemingly at their own wild will, peach trees and apricots, mulberries and maranelli, pears and apples.

The vines and fruit trees, like the statues, were mostly on the ground; but the orchard, where weeds or cabbages were not, was made lovely by the broad grey green leaves of artichokes.

The Venetian artichoke is *pur sang* a Venetian plant; easy to cultivate, easy to sell, and excellent to eat. The core has no choke, and can be swallowed whole. The crop is cut with any knife. The plant requires only that its roots should be covered by and heaped up with soil before the frosts, and uncovered after them. Worth as much

18

as two and three centimes each when scarce, they are sold at twenty to thirty centimes the hundred when full in season, and as each plant will yield some score of heads its owner wins his profit with small labour. Pietro and his family were the " Ortolani " of the garden. His Paron was a Greek who lived at Venice, and came every morning to get the *bessi* that Pietro's artichokes were sold for.

I fell at once in love. What a garden could be made of the abandoned orchard, what scope for planting, what an escape from constant idleness, what a relief from my lately loved mistress the lagoon, from whom my soul now turned in the ungrateful satiety of too long possession.

The next morning we went to meet the Greek, a Venetian so called, because his house was near the Church of the Greci.

To the natives of the Giudecca all are foreigners who are not Giudecchites. I once had a garden man, a native of neighbouring Murano, who left me because he was hunted when he went outside the garden by the Giudecca boys as a *Forresti*, and this Paron was a Greek. Well, it was all the same, Greek, Francese, Inglese; he was a foreigner, for he did not live on the Giudecca.

Pietro was right, his Paron was a Greek.

I asked if I could rent the garden? "No." "Well, a bit of it?" To oblige me, yes, he would let me the cypress plot (twenty yards square, out of some four acres). I said it was not much; and he, that the orto was very valuable; but he would let me the cypresses, and give me leave to walk about the orchard—a permission that did not cost him anything, for, as he saw, I could not walk. "How much?" "Would I give him a parola of how much I was ready to pay?" Then Eugenio said the parola must come from him. "Well, as I was ill, and he wished me well, and he would like to do the Signore a kindly action, therefore he would let him the plot for nine hundred lire." "My Signore is tired now," said Eugenio, and he took me away.

When out again in the lagoon Eugenio said, "*Lascia mi fare*, the brigand, that is what he pays, or ought to pay, for the whole garden." It was true; and as he didn't pay, the proprietor was as ready to sell as I to buy, and so we came to terms.

CHAPTER IV

T was the end of 1884. There was much to do, and we set at once to do it. The houses were repaired, and the boundary wall was made good. Half dead and useless trees were felled, dead wood cut out and young trees planted. All this

was very easy : something less so to restrain the cortellazzo that hung from the back of the blue waistcoat, for Pietro and his helpers declared nearly every tree to be useless, and all wood dead, that they might have the more to sell and burn.

Much less easy was it, the orchard being ours, to decide what to do with it. A brand new plan in the old ground was desecration, and we agreed to make such changes only as, consistent with the existing scheme, were needed to utilise and beautify it.

It was necessary, too, to have tender regard for the genius of the place. "All is fine that is fit." An Italian garden has found a home in many an English pleasaunce, indeed the Italian, or rather Roman garden, as old and older than the Plinies, was the model of some of our loveliest. But our individual taste loves vegetation as Nature grows it rather than as man clips it.

Suitable as is the evidence of man's art to such gardens as those of the Pamfili Doria or Albani Villas, indeed to any appurtenant to grand Italian palaces or Scottish castles, and charming as are cut yews or box trees in their proper places, as illustrations in *Country Life* so often show us, we thought it as out of character to dump them down in the Giudecca, and to trace winding paths in a Venetian orchard, as it would be to set an up-to-date water-colour in a Sansovino frame, or a Titian in a modern one.

The universal measure that rules at Venice is the square, and the square is never square. The houses and palaces were built along the banks following the devious course of the canals. The Grand Canal is a letter S writ large. The foundations of the buildings were laid on upright piles driven some forty feet deep along the margins; the frontage was square, more or less, as the curve of the bank where the palace rose was slight or rapid. The building itself ran as squarely backwards as the square of its neighbours on either side permitted, and to attain the utmost cubic space that he could on his expensive foundation the builder designed a square that is seldom as equilateral as it looks.

A GARDEN IN VENICE

The outcome of this regard for economy of space and *spese* is a most commodious house with scarcely a quite square room within it; and few things are cleverer in decoration than the way in which the old stucco artist adapted his square design to a room that was not so, and makes one lose the sense of unsquareness in both design and room. A big *sala* runs most times through the centre of the house from front to back, the rooms opening into it on either side, and at the back of very many of the old houses there greets you the lovely surprise of an old and generally abandoned garden.

The approach proper to a Venetian house is from the water. There are numberless small canals, or *rii*, that divide, cut up the city into blocks. Sometimes, where the blocks are large, there is a *campo* in the centre, and houses built around it. *Calle*, or small footways, run at the back of these; and, when the space is sufficient, at the back or side of the gardens attached to the houses. These gardens then were, and are, more or less square or oblong; forms that necessitated lines straight and intersecting. The man who had laid out our orchard had followed, indeed it was prescribed for him, this universal Venetian rule, and the invention of the pergola—the great inventor's name, alas, is lost to history—made it easy, practical, and beautiful.

As something is written nowadays in books and papers on the pergola, and many are put up in England, I may hazard a few observations on its use and possible abuse. If you buy a horse, is it to ride or drive? Some men take or seek a wife as a friend, a dear friend, constant, or occasional; some as a companion, a sweet companion, by day or night; some as a managing directress, and she oft becomes a tyrant; some as a servant, of whom they're apt to make a slave. So with the pergola; decide what you want it for, and the choice of one of its kind, or of none, is easy. In Italy we need it for the vine; in England it serves more often for the rose.

The pruning of a plant must depend upon its habit, and the amount of pruning must be in inverse ratio to its strength. A plant of strong growth hard-pruned will apply all its vigour to the making of more growth, and if continuously restrained and over-thwarted in its nature, it dies. A less vigorous plant will be aided by cutting back, to put the strength that is in it to the growth of flowers or fruit rather than of wood. The Italian vine, with its force of habit and ramping nature, cannot be treated as a French or German one, and cut down close to the soil. So in roses, strong climbers must be allowed to climb. But whilst the pergola is admirable in Italy for the vine, it is, it seems to me, little adapted to the rose.

For the vine, then, we want support in Italy, and are glad of shade. Beauty is of the essence of the place. All this the pergola gives us. Support may, it is true, be given by stakes or poles, with wires stretched like a fence along the rows of vines, but this way of training like a hedge gives no shade, and if simple and practical it has little charm, unless seen in ground, left open as a field, or laid out as an orchard rather than a garden.

28

A GARDEN IN VENICE

In a warm climate there are few things more enjoyable than a stroll, even in August, under a vine pergola. You walk in deep shade, the fierce sun held outside, the big bunches of grapes, black and purple, yellow and golden, all the promise of a rich harvest, hanging down to knock your hat, to blob your nose, feast your eye, and tempt your lips.

The rose, too, needs support, and this should be given so as to show the beauty of the plant and the redundance of its bloom. But under the pergola you see nothing but what you should not see; the unhealthy leaves, pining for light and air, and possibly an occasional blossom fading and colourless. The pendant growth of the grape brings its fruit into sight, the upward shoot of the rose carries its flowers out of touch and view. So that to see a rose, much more to pick one, you must go outside the pergola that holds it.

The support, then, in the nature of a pergola, best fitted for the rose is not a pergola but an arbour. Coming to such a leafy rose-house the wealth of blossom on either side, and even on the top, is in full view; even sitting within it the roses climbing up the entrance posts or columns, and hanging down the front, are within the easy reach of eye and hand. Prolong the arbour and it becomes a tunnel, and, as is the case with tunnels, the sooner one gets out of it and the less one sees of it the better pleased one may be.

CHAPTER V

HERE are three beautiful kinds of pergola that I know. Two others far less so. To dispose of these last first. The pergola is sometimes made of iron. The heat of the metal in a hot climate hurts the vine and its material offends the eye.

31

A GARDEN IN VENICE

Then there is wood sawn, and worse bepatterned. I was asked last year what should be done with such a one, that reminded me in the fashioning of its woodwork of decoration used in the South Sea Islands, and I curtly said, "Take it down." Two days afterwards I found it gone. There is some pleasure in giving advice that you are asked for if, when its worth is recognised, it is so quickly acted on. The other forms of pergola that I know, and that are practical and lovely, may be seen, amongst many other places, at Amalfi, Gravosa, and Venice.

At the convent hotel of Amalfi there are (happily not touched by the earth-slip of three years ago) large square columns built of stone and mortar with big wooden beams overhead. This solidity was very suitable to a place that might slip, and nothing can be more lovely than the effect of the heavy old grey-white pergolas from under the vines of which one looked along the terrace that stands hundreds of feet above the pretty Italian town and harbour, and the bright blue sea dotted with dots of sails

32

A GARDEN IN VENICE

As at Shakespear's Cliff, but with brighter colours—

> "The crows and choughs, that wing the midway air,
> Show scarce so gross as beetles."
> "The fishermen, that walk upon the beach,
> Appear like mice; and yon tall anchoring bark,
> Diminished to her cock; her cock a buoy
> Almost too small for sight: the murmuring surge
> That on the unnumbered idle pebbles chafes,
> Cannot be heard so high."

I have lately seen a pergola of masonry something similar at Venice in a garden bought by Lady Radnor. But there is only one line of columns, the crossbeams resting at the other side on the outer wall that protects the garden from the canal outside. The path underneath is paved and sunk some two feet below the surface of the ground and the result is charming.

At Gravosa, that most lovely place that stands on a bay back to back with Ragusa and its port, the road that joins the two towns runs over the promontory that rises between them, and along that road may be seen some mediæval, probably Greek pergolas, the whole in a scene of witching beauty. The supports are very ancient marble and stone columns not large nor high, but perfectly proportioned, serving well their purpose and in entire harmony with all around them.

The pergolas in general use at Venice are of other and very evanescent kind. The pollard willows that grow in the low lands of the neighbouring *terra-firma* supply the poles, and they are sold, according to their size, at from five francs to twenty the hundred. The initial cost is small, and so, well suited to Venetian habits; but it is not a cheap vine support, as the soft wood, quickly grown, quickly decays, and requires constant renewal. The upright *pali*, planted about two metres apart in a line on either side of the footway, are first connected with *cordoni*, as the laterals are called, at from five to eight feet from the ground, according to the strength of the vines and their owner's requirements for use or appearance. Then the two lines, six to eight feet apart, are joined and made interdependent by cross poles, *traversi*. On these traversi are laid two longitudinal lines constructed of the lighter poles, and

34

A PERGOLA AND LILIES.

the worn pali and cordoni judged not strong enough for their former service. In their place, to give more air and light, I now use lines of zinc wire. The whole is bound together by osier bands called *stroppe*, and secured against lateral wind pressure by buttress poles tied to every fourth or fifth upright.

The stroppe require renewal every two years, pali and cordoni every three to four, when the whole pergola is thrown down and remade. The vines, though often thrown to the ground too, in the erection of the pergola, do not suffer ; but when the cost of the labour is added to the price of pali and stroppe such a pergola is not in the long run cheap. If not so light and taking little space it is most appropriate and the effect is charming. In such a garden as ours the six or seven hundred yards of pergolas built on solid brick or stone pilasters would be utterly out of character, and so weighted might go through the bottom or sink with it into the lagoon we swim on.

Our pergolas then were there, and we too happy

to accept them in line and kind. But the spaces, the so-called squares they formed and enclosed, had to be dealt with. Many were small, filled with useless, dwarfed, and ugly fig-trees. The cabbages and potatoes, not too well grown, that filled others in due season, scarcely commended themselves to us as permanent inhabitants, and we called on our imagination and our memories for plans of betterment.

CHAPTER VI

HERE was a Ross-shire garden we had known and loved many years ago, that may be in much as unlike our present one as Scotland is to Italy, yet was in its laying out not unsimilar, and might give us a theme, as it were, on which to write in flowers our garden story. With the old castle wall to the north, and the ground sloping to the south, it was divided and protected from cold

37

winds by high cut hedges. Each division was subdivided by espalier hedges of pears and apples. Outside the espalier-formed squares were borders of flowers, and inside were currant, gooseberry bushes, and the ordinary plants of a kitchen garden. At its south boundary it had a ha-ha wall, with below a meadow and a trout stream.

Our Venice garden had the main features of the Scotch one. For the trout stream, that sparkling joy of life, we had, alas, a quiet substitute in the lagoon. But to our north was the high wall that once enclosing the Convent, that Casa di Chiesa, now shuts in the perhaps more useful Casa di Pena. Useful to society and useful to us, for, though it is sad for the bad ones in it to be constrained to silence, security from north wind and noise is a boon of great price to the garden and to us.

Of espaliers there were none, but they could be made, and in the meantime we had the vines to mark out and serve as a background to our garden plots. The borders of these could be given to flowers, and to Pietro and his waistcoat could be

38

left the inner squares. Setting to work on this plan, we planted pears to make espalier hedges and duly trained them. But the sun is too hot, at least on the southern exposure which we chose for them, killing them with the heat of its regard. Of the dozens of trees so planted a few only lived, either where they got some shade, or single trees that have been allowed to grow as Nature meant them.

The vines were at once taken in hand. One or two pergolas were suppressed where the vines were past recovery or weak, and one or two squares were thrown together ; thus in one case massing two tiny orchards of Marinelli, that looked at each other across the line of the vines they stifled. Then Furlani were called in, men who, passing the summer on the mountain slopes, leave their wives to the snows of winter, and come to Venice and the neighbouring towns to sell hot chestnuts or cooked pears, and to bake bread or make chocolate. Men of this kind are very frugal and industrious. They go to France and Germany in numbers to work at various trades, and return

when their pockets are full with hard-earned
economies. It is their ambition to buy a plot of
land and build a house for their wives and children. The children when they grow up bring
their wages to the home, and the fathers grown
old are so supported. At Belluno, where we
spend the summer, I have seen half a dozen of
such houses built in the last five or six years.
Each has its plot of ground for *grano turco*, and
often grass enough to keep a cow, and the price
of such lots is high.

One of these men who came to me was a very
able worker, not rare among them, but also an
honest worker, giving a fair day's work for his
day's pay; and this, being with me something
above the general rate, was a further temptation
perhaps to misconduct. Nevertheless, he ac-
counted to the last centime of the money he
spent, till at the end of his third season he disappeared, and I was told, the police wanting him,
he had gone to America. I sincerely trust he
met there with the fortune that his conduct with
me deserved. It was an erring cast of the police-

man's net that cost me a good man. A cast doubly erring, for it was too well made and its object badly chosen.   There are so many I know who might have been better wanted, and both less missed, and better missed at Venice.

By his help a couple of thousands of pali were bought and planted. The cordoni and traversi were prepared in length and shape where necessary, to render their tying easy. Many thousands of stroppe were sorted into sizes and lengths ; the large branches split, to be put in use where greater strength was needed, the smaller and shorter to tie the vines to the pergola framework.

Next, the paths were made, and mindful of Hyde Park, boat-loads of sea shells were brought from the Lido as substitutes for, and improvement on, the gravel that the Veneto does not furnish. The paths were then bordered with box or old bricks. The last the best, for bricks, especially the old ones, are not unsightly, want no trimming, take nothing from the soil, harbour no insects, and hold rather than consume the precious moisture.

A GARDEN IN VENICE

Then the borders were planted, not an easy task, for one side of the pergola running, as ours mostly do, east and west, is in the shade. Sometimes too the pergolas are doubled to meet the exigencies of some extra vigorous vines, and few herbaceous and seedling plants will submit gracefully to be deprived of so much light and air. It took then some time to fill them, and it takes some thought to keep them filled, but nothing is more marvellous than the growth and multiplication of plants in Venice that are pleased with Venice. And here a word must be said on the peculiarities of Venice gardening, bound up, as these are, with its pains and pleasures.

There is no other soil and climate so full of whim and fantasy. You buy a score of magnolias, trees that you see growing luxuriantly in other Venice gardens. One of your score alone will perhaps thrive. You plant a dozen roses of the same kind, bought from the same rose garden; this and that plant will ramp, the rest not move. Your efforts to fill the garden is a story of failures, and yet the successes thrive so fast that the

42

PERGOLA AND OLD GATEWAY.

scissors and knife and billhook must be kept at work to let in air and sunlight.

After a time our thick heads found out one cause of failure. The soil is made; brought in boats from pulled down houses or dust heaps, or from the bottom of dredged canals. One rose you plant may have the luck to light on an ancient dung heap, the next vainly strive to root in the scorched *débris* of some long-forgotten fisher's kitchen. Again, the soil on the surface may be sweet and wholesome, but all plants that have tap-roots, or seek deep feeding, would find at some three feet down salt earth or even salt water. I have seen in a very hot and dry summer the surface in places white with a salt efflorescence drawn up by the power of the sun.

Peach trees, therefore, have so short a lifetime that I have renewed them twice and some even three times already. Nor does cutting their tap-root before planting add materially to their endurance. Only lateral root running trees can live to full age. So our Marinelli last, lovely with white flowers or red fruit each in its season, and the mulberries see out generations of Furlani.

These mulberries are a source of income. We have five trees large and wide-spreading. In their season, July, they are purple black with delicious fruit, their branches so laden that they are sometimes broken with the weight. When I bought the garden I found that a family of Furlani came yearly from the mountains of Friuli, paying a rent of seventy lire for the right to pick and sell the fruit—first, however, providing a supply for the master's use. In addition to money they bring, a relic perhaps of the old payment in kind, two mountain cheeses, bound up in green-leaved boughs—one of fresh hard creamy curd, that is generally eaten with sugar, the other smoked and seasoned. I would not disturb their tenancy, and the children of those days now carry on the trade their father is no longer fit for.

To pick the fruit is a stainful task that requires skill. Unless well plucked a nearly empty skin remains in the bungler's hands. The juice has spurted on his arms and face and clothes.

44

A GARDEN IN VENICE

Among our young women visitors are some who are fond of mulberries, and we advise the prettiest ones to pick with their lips. This may be, and often is successfully done, but not always, as lips with teeth no longer white, and tips, stained dark red, of upturned tilted noses so often show. There are simple ways, as old perhaps as the days of Adam, of getting rid of stains on pretty lips; but the frocks, and it's well worth knowing, will only yield the colour that betrays their mistress's fancy to the smoke of burning sulphur. So even the oldest habit may be worth repeating and the commonest match have a merit of its own.

The Feast of the Redentore is the mulberry sacrifice or triumph. It is held on the third Saturday and following Sunday of July. A couple of days before we have a visit from the monks of the Monastery of the Redentore, who seek our flowers and fruit. We give them branches of either, with which are made large garlands of Mantegna type for the decoration of the church and doorway. These mendicants, for they are

45

of the Franciscan order, are, in the language and experience of the Fondamenta, *Buona gente*.

Begging with us at home is not a high ideal nor a meritorious practice, but then we have a poor law. In a land where no Elizabeth ever signed a law to prevent the starvation of her meanest subject, 'tis wonderful that those who by sickness, laziness, or incapacity run off the course, can eat enough to live. The kindness of the people to the people is wonderful. Of the service of the children to their parents I shall speak later. The charity of the well-to-do to the poorly off is great, the bequests of the dying, or the fearful, to make their peace with purgatory are many, but still there are hundreds with no kith or kin placed well enough to help them who would starve but for such men as these monks.

The Father Superior is an acquaintance I gladly see. Tall, gaunt, and handsome, in his brown frock he reminds one of a Ribera picture, and he is gentle in his voice and manner, unremitting in his quest, untiring in his labour.

46

OUR FONDAMENTO AND THE RIO DELLA CROCE.

A GARDEN IN VENICE

We have Cucine Economiche at Venice and on the Giudecca, which do much good, but the Redentore monk is not behind in the same service. The Padre and his fellows go out far and near, as do their brother monks of San Francesco nel Deserto, collecting everything that can help their poor, excepting money.

One summer evening years ago we had a picnic dinner at San Francesco with many other residents and friends. It came on to storm and the party sought refuge, that was most kindly given, in the part of the monastery that women are allowed to enter. It was proposed by one who knew much of monks, as he knew of many things in Italy, Spain, and the East, to make a collection that would show some return for the hospitality we had received. But the money for the monks' distribution to their poor, that we should have been glad to leave behind, had to be taken to Venice and spent in provisions before it could be accepted.

One day, some time ago, I was told at Salce near Belluno, sixty miles away, where we pass the hot part of the summer, that a Venetian acquaintance wished to see me. It was my Padre of the Giudecca. He was carrying a sack half full of white beans with which to make the soup so freely given in the winter to the Venetian poor, and asked my help to fill it from our farm produce.

On the Saturday, the eve of the Redentore festa, all Venice, poor and rich, gentle and simple, spend their night abroad. From dark to dawn the Giudecca quays, called Fondamente, are crowded with sightseers and pleasure-wooers of every age and size and sex. Among them the Furlani have a ready sale for their fruit. For there are few on bank or boat who do not eat that night of mulberries.

On the canal thousands of boats pass up and down the water, most, if not all, decked with awnings or shelters built of green boughs and flowers, hung with lanterns of every shape, device, and colour, laden with suppers of all degrees of merit, and crowded with families, or parties, of quality as varied. The girls and boys, the women and the men seem, and do, I believe, eat all night;

48

the babies refuse their mothers' breasts for their fathers' glasses, and why every one, or at least very many, do not burst and die is a mystery. Or is it a miracle to be ascribed to the Church of the Redentore?

Nothing noisy or unpleasant, however, happens to them as far as I have heard or seen; and *faute de miracle*, it may be the distraction of the bands of music in barges or on the Fondamenta, and the firework displays, that give them pause and us immunity.

An hour or two before dawn very many of the Redentore votaries leave the Giudecca for the Lido. One night we went too, and 'twas one of the strangest sights a long life has shown me.

At our supper was a capital young fellow, with, by-the-bye, a story to his credit, who had been sent by Armstrong's firm to put up a huge crane at the Arsenal. It was proposed by some wild tiptilted one that we should go in my steam launch to the Adriatic outside and see what was to be seen on the Lido shore. My engineer was naturally not to be found, engaged as he probably was in eating the fifth hour of his supper on or under the seat of some family boat. But our Armstronger volunteered to light the fire, and stoke and drive, and so we went.

It was a lovely morning as I steered in the clear night light through, and then away from, the crowds of boats, and running alone out to sea at San Nicoletto, we steamed gently along the Lido eastern shore.

Dawn broke as we got abreast the bathing-places, and we saw a dark line stretching along the sands, say perhaps a quarter of a mile in length. We ran in to some sixty yards or so from this line, and saw it was composed of people motionless and silent, two or three in depth. The dawn got lighter, and I turned to see in the east behind me the first ray of the sun rising from the Adriatic. Attracted by a noise, a rustle, and a hum, I looked back shorewards. The dark line had become pink and white. As the first ray of the sun struck the water, as much of every man's or woman's clothes as the law permitted was left at their feet, and with a rush the peace

of the calm poetic sea was broken by the splash
and frolic of a thousand bathers.

It must have been the sun that coloured our
faces and called out such ohs of unfeigned amaze-
ment, that Armstrong forgot his engine, and the
tilted tip changed for the moment its tempting
charm for rigid straightness. To avoid the per-
manence of so dire a calamity I turned the boat's
head for home.

CHAPTER VII

GARDEN is not made in a year; indeed it is never made in the sense of finality. It grows, and with the labour of love should go on growing.

There are old gardens that one might fear to touch, and yet I suppose that the most devout and respectful worshipper and worker in one who really loved it would leave some impress on it.

There are others made *di nuovo*, and on these the owner may let his fancy run, or call in the aid of the high priests of gardening, who, with dogmatic confidence, tell us what is wrong and what is right. And there are some like the garden of our story, for which the main design has already long been drawn, with full scope left for filling in details.

To achieve this worthily, we called up memory in aid of our conception and borrowed from the gardens we had seen. I have said how we got help from distant Ross-shire for the general plan. We turned to it again for the completion of the picture, getting other ideas, however, from Battaglia, close at hand; and from gardens as far apart in distance, climate, and *mise en scène* as Hampton Court and the gardens of the Moorish Generaliffe at Granada.

One or two of the squares, formed in accordance with the Scottish design, were at once stolen from Pietro's vegetables and laid out in rose gardens. Year after year the same theft was made until we were obliged to stop, not for kitchen needs, or less love of roses, or from lack of other varieties to add to those we have, but that we thought, and think, the mixture of the useful with the beautiful gives the latter greater value.

For this same reason of utility lawns were made of several other former cabbage plots to serve as places where in summer heats we sit.

On one such lawn two huge mulberry trees grow, said to have four hundred years of age, with at one corner a large bay. These bays are very picturesque. They were not above a few feet in height when we bought the garden, being cut each year and their branches sold, either as evergreens at Christmas or for use in laundries. We have saved them from further robbery, and many of them are now really fine features among the trees. The trunks, possibly from having been cut in old times, grow as the hazels and ashes and birches in English copses that are cut for faggots every fourteen or fifteen years, and have a dozen silvery· stems growing close together. These running up into the dense covering of the dark green leaves they nourish, give an evergreen and southern look; indeed, they are only second to the cypresses in their height and beauty.

Two other small lawns were made as the ground plan of some oleanders; one of these shrubs, not less than thirteen or fourteen feet in height, and as many in breadth, is, in July, one mass of bright red flower. Others are red and pink, ot various tints, and pale yellow and pure white.

Round and on these lawns, too, are Japanese kaki, the only magnolia I can get to grow, and pomegranates. The kaki and the small Japanese maples are worth a place in any garden. The last are slow in growing; but the kaki shows more than mere contentment with its new home by the vigour of its growth, the masses of its beautiful glossy dark foliage, and the size and quantity of its luscious golden orange fruit.

Of the pomegranates we have several kinds. It is the common one that gives the fruit, so dear to old designers on wood and canvas, and in

AN OPEN SPOT.

marble, stone, and metal. Other species have double flowers, red, red and white, and white; the first two grow luxuriantly and are beautiful.

I might here mention a peach that, new to me, was brought us from Valdobiadene, near Feltre. The flower is very double, and a lovely red colour. The fruit, for, unlike many double-flowering trees, it fruits freely, is of a double form, such as one sees occasionally in a sport of plums.

At Battaglia we had seen a wondrous China rose hedge, high and thick, one mass of bloom and loveliness. In partial imitation, and perhaps in betterment, as far as material goes, we planted a hedge of that dearest and sweetest of roses, the old cabbage, on either side of a vine pergola more than a hundred and fifty yards long. Our lines of cabbage roses do not grow thick and high as the Battaglia China, and it is high praise to say of any rose that it can be better for the purpose of a hedge than a really good specimen of Bengaliensis; but in late May or early June, when other roses are for the moment going off betwixt their blowing seasons, this pergola is very charming, and carries on our bloom with the help of the iris, Canterbury bells, larkspurs, foxgloves, &c., to the madonna lilies, whose flower-time theirs overlaps.

The idea taken from Hampton Court was not successful. I remembered half a century ago some beds there surrounded by a hedge of Devoniensis roses. With us, though offered many sites, Devoniensis will not grow. For reasons of soil and climate, given later, the refusals of certain plants to be transplanted are with us much too common. We console ourselves that, if their love be not for me, some other love there'll surely be.

The idea we borrowed from the Generaliffe was the fashion of a tank. Few places are better able to give advice on this crucial subject for a garden than the Alhambra hill. Standing in a torrid climate, and dry and springless in itself, finishing off a promontory five hundred feet above Granada, it would be barren but for the engineering care and skill of the thirteenth century Moors. As it is, their work is still in being, and rills of sparkling water, brought in

58

A GARDEN IN VENICE

conduits, generally invisible, give drink and life to lovely gardens.

There was one there, El Hacir del Gran Capitan, a tiny house, the passage between it and its kitchen roofed by a huge vine, and a small garden of some seven terraces, each composed of the sustaining wall of the one above it, two narrow flower borders, a path between them, and a fountain with an open conduit carrying the water to the basin lower down.

The garden itself, and then Granada below, and then the Vega, as the plain is called, with the Guadalquivir shimmering in silver bends amongst green meadows, grey trees, and small hills or hillocks, each giving standing-room to the village and the church, and perhaps the convent; at the end of all, rising in the intense blue sky, the snows of the Sierra Nevada. That view and the Museo del Prado pictures are the wonders of old Spain.

From the larger garden of the Generaliffe we copied a tank for holding water, but this expensive subject must be dealt with later.

H 2

59

CHAPTER VIII

ROBABLY the joy of a garden lies, more or less, in its wealth; one loves to see things grow as if they liked it. To see colour in masses, depth of shade, bloom in profusion, glorious promise, and bountiful flowering— these are the characteristics that the soil of the *Tomba dei Fiori* will give to those who ask it. It is well, no doubt, where Nature is more frugal, to plant beds and borders with many different sorts of flowers; with paint-box in hand to study precisely

the contrasts and juxtaposition of plants and tints, and so to plan and grow a very lovely and finished picture.

This is as a Meissonier to a Tintoretto. But Tintoret is the better master for Venice. The extent is ample, the borders many and long, the separate divisions of beds are numerous, and a bigger brush can be filled with fuller colour and the plants planted in larger masses.

In Italy, too, flowers grow and multiply in a way unknown to England, and it is wise to take advantage of Nature's bounty.

As the cabbage and artichokes of our prepossessors gave way to the daffodils, anemones, and tulips mostly brought from Holland, the produce of these bulbs yearly made demand for greater space. Small islets of foxgloves or columbines or larkspurs spread themselves into continents, and a splash of Love in the Mist flowed over into a sea of blue. The vigour, too, of the plants that love the soil is so great that to reduce them and their groups to the dimensions that are observed in what is called a well-kept garden

NATURE'S BOUNTY.

would be to restrain their nature, and we mostly
prefer to let them ramp. As much as possible
we give Nature her head, and when she is ridden
it is with the lightest snaffle.

The result is that from early spring to late
autumn we see a mass of bloom. The daphne
tells us spring has come, and we are snow white
with Marinelli, the only cherry which will stand
our salt air and soil. Then pink with peach
blossom, sweet with lilac, gay with may, For-
sythia, Deutsia, Spirea, Weigelea, and Azalea.
A laburnum, the only one we could persuade to
grow, reminds one of the Derby, and wistaria
disputing with roses the clothing of our cottages,
climbs to the top of tall trees to deck with flowers
the leaves of Chionanthus. A little later Pitto-
sporum with shining dark foliage and white
intensely daphne-scented flowers, quits shrub size
to figure as a tree—one I know reaches the second
storey of a neighbouring palace—and Rhincos-
pernum hides the stone garlands of our modest
Venus, runs over the Faun that stands near by,
and helps to hide a cottage front. Whilst the

63

bower that stretches between the statues is a
purple glory of Clematis Jackmanni.

Before this the garden is white and gold with
daffodils that, blossoming with the Marinelli,
blow on to greet the roses—the Emperor, Em-
press, and Sir Watkin only yielding in size and
beauty to the well-named Incomparable Sulphur
Phœnix, with a flower larger and sweeter than
the gardenia it resembles; and our dozen rose
gardens are carpeted with tulips and anemones.

We have found it answer to mix standard roses
with the bush ones, the shade of the tall plants
giving some shelter to the dwarfer ones from the
hot summer sun. For the same reason it has
succeeded extremely well to plant tulips and anemones and even strawberries among the roses.
Of course the ground plants are planted thinly.
And a rose-bed carpeted with Cardinal and Rose
de Nice, or with the Caen or Chrysanthemum
Anemones, is very lovely. It is delightful, too,
to pick one's strawberries and cut one's tea rose
from the same bed.

When the tulips are nearly over the Iris come

64

in. Of these we have a great profusion. Purple, pale blue, and white, bronze and yellow, Florentine, English and German, Spanish and Japanese. In a long border that joins one side of the cherry orchard large groups of different kinds are growing, and when in flower they so fill the eye that as one looks up the border more than a hundred yards long, leading to the square of the cherry orchard, it seems one continuous mass of their bloom. Round three sides of this orchard there is little else except some lilies of the valley, the offshoots as it were of the fourth side, which is filled with them growing beside and under cabbage roses.

These delicious so-called lilies make full return for our love and small demand upon our care. It is an amusement for young women in the spring to pick them in large bunches, or rather to pull them, for the lily flower stalk should be pulled out of its socket, never broken. To favour this pastime and for ourselves, we have four or five plots some ten to fifteen yards long in the transverse borders; the sites chosen so as to prolong as much as possible the flowering season. It is necessary to change a bed in rotation nearly every year, for they grow so thick that the leaves suffocate the flowers. The first year they do little, the next two or three they bloom profusely, and the next more poorly. The double flowering plants, less social, require more space. They seem to do best dispersed about in small colonies, or singly, in places generally chosen by themselves, or moved to, aided by accident or perhaps by birds.

In May, early and mid, comes our great show, the roses. We have very many kinds, but we love best those that love us best, and are rather fond of putting a good many of any of the varieties that blow most freely in a mass, trying as to place to suit their idiosyncrasies. A large group of Comte de Paris, or Papa Gontier, in the shade they seek; or of Beauté Inconstante, Madame Jules Grolez, Maria Immaculata, in the sun they revel in. Further, there are so many roses, such as Gustave Regis, Souvenir de Catherine Guillot, Madame Eugène Resal, and her elder sister,

66

A GARDEN IN VENICE

Madame Laurette Messimy, Comtesse Riza du Parc, Caroline Testout, Madame Falcot, and the old Malmaison, and that sweetest of roses, La France, which, seeming to the climate born, give us flowers in such rich masses that we rather give up trying to grow the more fickle or contradictory, beautiful as they may be. Madame Hoste is unkind, but I hope to overcome her coyness. La Marque, Devoniensis, and Niphetos will have none of us. I am sorry, but as from April generally to Christmas, and sometimes to the Russian New Year's Day, we can cut from thousands of plants of hundreds of varieties that thrive with us, we may well be and are content.

Standard, pillar, and climbing roses revel in Venice air. I once counted a thousand blooms on a Maréchal Niel that, grafted on a Banksia, covered an old cow-house. Alas, the effort was too much for the tree, and it died. The Marshal we find capricious, he will not grow on his own roots, and is rather difficult to please as to place. Well suited in this respect he is Napoleonic.

Most useful roses for pillars or post, for arbour

A GARDEN IN VENICE

or hedges, are Madame Abel Carriere, Aimée Vibert, Madame Bérard (her mother, Gloire de Dijon, grows thick and imperfect flowers), Reine Olga de Wurtemburg, Gloire Lyonnaise, and Céline Forrestier, in full sun, Rêve d'Or and William Allen Richardson in half-shade. Shade, that is, from sun, not light. All roses here, as I suppose everywhere, do best in full light, though some cannot resist our sun; and crave full open air, whilst needing protection from wind.

Another pull we have in Venice is that the colour of some roses, said to be doubtful in England, is in our fine weather immaculate. Our Crimson Rambler, for instance, grows on grafted stock magnificently. The stretch it covers is enormous, the growth astounding, the bloom profuse, and the colour, even to the last, the truest crimson. It must, however, have free air and full sun. Planted in a place ever so little shaded from light and air it grows moderately, the leaves are often yellow, and its colour faulty. Reine Marie Henriette, sometimes reckoned a coarse rose in England, has with us the same

68

merits and requirements, and blooms too, early and late.

The roses that will grow on their own roots we prefer so grown. The system of reproduction called *Margotti* is general in Italy, and renders this mode of cultivation easy. Less known in England I may describe it for amateurs. The simplest way is with small cornucopias of zinc, in form as the paper ones the grocers fill with pennyworths of sugar, only open at the bottom; or with four to five inch pots having a slit in the side. In July a branch of the new but well-ripened wood of the rose to be reproduced is surrounded by the zinc or passed through the slit in the pot, a cut being first made under a bud. The pot or zinc is then filled with fine ordinary earth, or earth with sand, and tied for support to a small cane or stake, then covered with moss to prevent evaporation, and kept moderately moist. In about eight weeks the branch is cut from underneath its cradle, the contents taken out without disturbance, and the plant well rooted, potted. The young plants then pass the winter out of doors,

in any place protected from cold winds and shel-
tered from frost by a covering of leaves or of
moss or fine fodder. I have found this better
than sinking the pot in the soil, which with us,
perhaps owing to the salt it contains, is very cold
in winter. Roses so made gain a full year on
those taken from cuttings, and are strong flowering plants by the next early summer. Most
varieties also last, and in all ways do so much
better than plants grafted on any stock that we
layer as soon as may be the many roses we get
from Lyons or elsewhere, earthing up the plant to
near the graft and bending one or more branches
under the soil, to root.

In late May we have the lilies. *Lilium candidum*,
the only one of the genus that takes to us kindly,
borders our pergolas in such tall quantities that
the anniversary of their patron, Saint Antonio of
Padua, the thirteenth of June, is made lovely by
day and bright by night with the light of the
virgin flowers. On some evenings they even
drive us from the garden by their overwhelming
scent. They require re-planting with change of

RAKING COSMOS.

place every half-dozen years, and in fresh soil
grow so grandly that we have often heads of
fifteen, sixteen, and even twenty flowers on a
single stem, of sometimes $5\frac{1}{2}$ feet high.

We used to fill our borders and other beds
with summer plants and annuals. This we have
given up, as we migrate in July with the swallows
to the mountains. Coming back to the late part
of our vintage we strive to be reconciled for the
cutting of our grapes by the money they bring
in, and to accept as the glory of the garden the
white and pink flowers of the raking cosmos, the
scarlet of the amaranthus and salvias, the autumn
roses, and the chrysanthemums that grow in
glorious profusion of all colours.

There has been a great improvement in the
fruit of Venice since we've known it, in obedience
to the law of constant progress that happily pre-
vails despite the doubts of the soured or unhappy.
A pear was unknown other than the small brown
native which ripened and decayed in August.
Now from trees brought from Milan we gather
grand fruit of the names best known in exhibi-

tions, and eat delicious pears from July to May. The figs were prized for their size; now we have three or four kinds notable for their excellence in taste. Of grapes I write later; suffice it now to say that if not so large as those growing in English hothouses, ours will yield to none in flavour. The strawberries were of the woodland without the woods that gave them their food and shelter; now we have them of good size and quality, though curiously the several varieties we have imported have merged their differences and agreed to make one first-rate family. Just as English and other races have founded across the ocean that excellent human type, the American.

Raspberries will not bear our whiff of the sea, but gooseberries give us tarts when tiny, and are less crude than the fruit grown at home. When ripe in July they are neglected, for there is so much fruit that is better. Currants, white, red, and black, are great bearers. Of apples on the Giudecca we only know the flower, though on the island of Sant Erasmo near by, some trees own do fairly well. Peaches are excellent. Years ago the fruit that bore the name had a hard yellow flesh that clung to its skin, and uncooked was uneatable. Now it would be difficult to find better peaches of sorts early, mid, and late from July to October. Apricots are plentiful but not so very good. I suppose they ripen too quickly to get the mellow flavour of an English wall-grown apricot; and nectarines will not grow.

Plums of very many sorts are unrivalled. My youth remembers at home the joy of the green-gage; the lesser pleasure of a well-ripened egg plum when you found one; and the wholesome tartness of a wine-sour tart. This last we have not. I believe out of Yorkshire it is difficult to find, but with us the sun does the cooking of kinds that are similar: the egg plum is always ripened, the greengage is a delight, and a dark sister, the black gage, dark blue without and golden green within, is in the fulness of flavour as a brunette of the south to a flaxen-coloured German. We have, too, the golden drops, each one mouthful of sun sugared plum excellence; amoli, suchetti, and many others all of merit.

A GARDEN IN VENICE

Of fruit less known there are the Kaki and
Nespolo that come from Japan. The last is very
good in early spring; they ripen in Venice as
late as May. And the Kaki is a golden bag of
sugar in November and December; too sweet for
me, but those that like them like them greatly.
Then there are melons of many sorts and great
excellence. They seem, however, to require
early renewal from their parent stock. The fruit
grown from the seeds that come to us from
England lose in a year or two their respective
characters. Even Bacirro, the great yellow melon
of the Greek archipelago, has a tendency to
round his long form and fatten. The Egyptian
water-melon, Anguria, is much grown, but those
who have crushed its red flesh like frozen snow
in the desert heat, would scarcely recognise the
Venetian temperate produce.

Our fruit then is abundant and excellent, as it
should be in a temperature where it should form,
and does form, a large part of one's daily diet.
And then the price brings it happily within
the reach of the poorest. Our surplus fruit is

74

A GARDEN IN VENICE

considerable, and we sell in their full season the
Marinelli cherries at five centimes, *i.e.*, a halfpenny, the kilo of $2\frac{1}{4}$ lbs. Grapes at times as
low as eight centimes the kilo ; peaches eight to
ten centimes the kilo. Pears, such as one used
to pay one and even two francs apiece for at
Paris, at twenty to thirty centimes the kilo ; and
delicious figs at thirty centimes the hundred. A
huge melon, an excellent supper for four people
with bread, sells for ten centimes. Thus a
Venetian, be he Gondolier or Conte, may, and
often does in summer time, eat healthily at small
cost. The people's fire is rarely lit more than
once a day, when the polenta, made of maize
flour, is cooked in sufficient quantity to be eaten
hot at midday, cold at dusk. Sometimes even the
ever-present polenta is dispensed with, and the
outlay on the fire which is not laid out will
almost pay for the bread bought to take polenta's
place.

For twopence, too, you may make a beggar
happy. Fifteen to twenty figs at five centimes,
fifteen centimes of bread, and a generous penny

K 2

75

more will buy him from a glass to a pint of wine, or, what he will like better, a glass of *graspa*, the spirit they distil here from the wine lees, and love.

CHAPTER IX

HE vintage is, as they say here, an *affare serio*, and, like all affairs, it may be good or bad or indifferent. Some years ago the gross yield was less and less evenly distributed. The diseases, if not fewer, were more confined to the vineyards badly cultivated,

whose consequent smaller produce made the prices better for the cultivators of those that, taken better care of, gave also the better yield. So that the profits gained by the few were increased, as is often the case, by their neighbours' loss.

Now the culture of the vine is better understood. A liberal and timely use of sulphate of copper and of sulphur combats the diseases. The commercial want of combination of Italy with France and Germany prevents the sending, as was once done, of large quantities of grapes to make Bordeaux or Rhenish wines, and the result is that too large quantities are thrown on the home market, with a corresponding fall in prices.

We have several kinds of eating grapes, " Uva di Tavola," amongst others two or three sorts of Muscats, black and white, and a black and a white Lugliatico, an early grape, as the name denotes, something like the old English Sweetwater, a Cenerentola, a Meran, and Uva d'Ora. These used to sell at what I called the fair price

VINES AND LILIES.

of a penny to twopence a pound ; but the prices are now so low, especially in good seasons, that, as with English fruit, the culture does not always pay.

At Venice, too, if the table grapes, not grown in too large quantities, can make a price, low though it may be, the wine grapes are worse off, for the wine made at Venice matures in six months, and will not, in my experience, keep. Wine forced on the market was being sold this last spring at fifteen centimes the litre, or one penny halfpenny the quart.

The old garden, without the Sacca extension to be later spoken of, gave me for some years annually more than five tons of grapes. This paid when sold at an average of five to six farthings the pound ; but for a year or two our yield has been much diminished and the prices lowered. The beginning of the decadence in yield was one of the hail-storms that are the flail of Italy. We were in the garden one late July afternoon when a heavy storm attacked us. There was just time to seek shelter in the teahouse before the hail began. Then, with a scream, the storm burst on us ; hailstones fell for five to six minutes, many the size of partridge eggs, but mostly of a flatter form. In that short time we saw the vines almost denuded of leaves ; the grapes, nearly fit for picking, cut to the ground ; the garden bloom of course destroyed, and the paths covered with the hailstones that had done such savage mischief. It was a dreadful scene of garden devastation. Nor was the immediate effect the last ; the heavier stones so cut and bruised the rods which should the next years have borne the grapes that succeeding crops were greatly injured. On *terra-firma* many attempts have been made to drive the hail-storms off by cannon fire, and to the solution of the question the Government has lent its aid, but it is not yet decided whether the result is worth the powder.

These storms are very ·partial. The one I speak of did not break a pane of glass at Venice, and left untouched some gardens within a quarter of a mile of ours. By others I have known all unprotected windows at Venice smashed and our garden uninjured. Fortunately for us, the mainland suffers much more than we do. The storms seem to be less bad near the sea and near the mountains, worse in the intermediate plain.

With occasional hail-storms, ever-present disease, cost of material, of labour, and low prices, the vine-grower's budget is not likely to show a large surplus. To set his mind at rest as to the paying probabilities of his vineyard the Government steps in. Land is very highly taxed; our inner garden of about four acres pays two hundred and sixty francs a year. At the market the grapes are taxed 10 per cent. by that honest broker, the licensed go-between, and before they are cut in Venice their amount is estimated by a Government official and charged at the rate of six francs ninety-five centimes the quintale of a hundred kilos. Last year was an abundant year, the grapes were not of first quality, and I sold many quintali at ten francs, some at eight. Should the reader ask where

the profit comes in, the answer is that it is found
in the shade and the beauty of the pergolas, and
is satisfactory and great.

CHAPTER X

 GARDEN would be an arid waste without water, and before buying ours I had made inquiries as to the supply. I was shown the well in the cortile in front of the Palazzina. Its mouth was nearly flush with the ground, and as I could see through the

iron guard running round it that the water was nearly level with the mouth, and Pietro put a stick down to show its depth of nearly four yards, I accepted the assurance that there was always plenty. One thirsty day, when the garden was already ours, I asked for a glass of water. I got it, and with a very wry face began to learn how Venice of old was watered. It cost a good bit of money before I had completed my education and provided the garden with the supply it needed.

In the old days a hole was dug in the courtyards of the palaces, say, as in our case, ten yards by five, and ten feet deep. The sides and bottom of this were lined by clay about two feet thick. In the centre of this so formed basin a *canna*, or round chimney, say four to five feet across, was built of brick ; the lowest yard left pervious without mortar that the water might pass through to the upper part, made solid with cement. The whole basin was then filled with sand ; and pipes led into small chambers constructed of open brickwork in this sand, from

84

THE PALAZZINA AND A VERA DI POZZO.

the gutters of the palace roof, the rain that fell there.

The sand, I was told, occupied no space, *i.e.*, the well basin would hold almost as much water when filled with sand as when empty. It filtered the rain, and this passed, so filtered, through the lower pervious tier of bricks, and rose within the canna to the height of the water in the sand outside it. The water was drawn from the well by throwing down a secchio with a rope, and the blow of these secchi aërated the water. So the Venetian got his drink fresh from heaven, pure and sparkling, with no trouble but that of sending his womenfolk to fetch it. But if in a long summer the rain was forgetful and the women drew the well dry, the clay dried also ; cracked, as the rude manner of dry clay is ; salt water from outside came to the rescue of the clay and the spoiling of the well.

This had happened in our cortile. So we had to call cunning well-makers to our aid. They first cleared the well basin of the sand, then cut the clay wall down inch by inch, patted it, talked to it, covered it with mats, and left it till the next morning to see if any drop of outside salt water, *la goccia*, as their head man called it, might come through despite the talking to and patting. This pretty play went on for weeks in a way that would have delighted the British Union workman's heart until the cutting and paring had nearly reached the bottom of the well, and quite passed the limits of our patience. Seeing us thoroughly out of temper, the cunning men built up the clay wall again with clay fresh from the mainland, much patted and befashioned it, built anew the canna, filled the basin with sand, and did not wait for the rain to say how elever they were, what a splendid well they'd made, and how cheap I ought to think their outrageous bill.

The water supply of old Venice, by means of these wells, was by no means bad as long as the clay walls held good. In long droughts only it was insufficient, and water was brought in barges from the neighbouring rivers, the Brenta or the Sile. Now, the supply is excellent. A number

A GARDEN IN VENICE

of artesian wells have been sunk on *terra-firma* at the base of the Euganean hills. The water passes direct from the wells into tubes, which, laid under ground and the Lagoon, carry the supply to a reservoir at S. Andrea, and from thence to the public wells and private houses of all Venice. The water is of the best and the supply sufficient.

It is a great gain to the comfort, cleanliness, and the health of the town; paid for by private consumers at six francs the ton, and alas, by all, with the loss of the Bigolante. These women were so called from the Bigol or yoke on their shoulders on which the bright copper secchi were hung, and came from near Udine or Belluno. They wore the mountain dress: a low soft black felt hat with silk cord and tassel; a full white chemise, with a sleeveless bodice and skirt of dark blue or green. It was their work to fill their secchi at the Pozzi Publici, and incidentally to add to the picturesqueness of the streets as they carried the water to many houses that had no wells of their own but could afford the service of the Bigolante and desired it. Into such houses now the water from the mainland is carried, and the streets are without one more of the decorative mementos of the past.

The use of water has a future in the Veneto. The water-power of the rivers is already used in many of the smaller towns to supply electric light, and the torrent of Cellina will shortly give its aid to light Venice at a very low price, and to work by electricity a number of the small machines that carry on the handicrafts.

The well we made on the ancient system answered for a time, but was insufficient for our needs, and after a year or two I remembered the cistern in the garden of the Generaliffe. A deep stone basin with marble cornice, some twenty yards long by five, if my memory is approximately right; with a grass border next the cornice and almost flush therewith; then a path, then borders of flowers on either side sloping to the path, and a temple building at the end. I followed the plan as regards the grass border, path, and flower borders; but as these got filled

88

THE VASCA GRANDE.

with bush and standard roses, the long continuous border of the Generaliffe got cut up into small beds by transverse paths for the convenience of tending and picking the roses. Standing back in each corner, the better to remind us of Spain, is a Chamoerops palm, grown now into trees more than twenty feet in height. Some bamboos too throw shadows on the water, and leaving out the temple that I could not copy, I have replaced it at either end by a rose-clad felse, as they call a tunnelled bower here, of at one end Celine Forrestier, and at the other some climbing Devoniensis, that have now ceded the place to Reine Marie Henriette. The sunny side of the Celine Forrestier is, when in bloom, a sight to see.

To make the reservoir or *vasca* the earth was excavated for the dimensions above given to a depth of six feet. About two feet below the surface the earth proper gave place to brick rubbish, showing that the way of reclamation I had afterwards a painful chance of seeing, was carried out by the fathers of Venice as it is now

M   89

by their descendants. At four feet down the earth was moist. A little more and it drained in so quickly at high tide, although the site was fifty yards inland, that a pump had to be kept at work to dry the excavation. Arrived four or five inches below the required six feet the bottom was levelled, then covered with larch boards, and on these was laid in cement a course or two of bricks. The end and side walls when built up on this foundation to eight or ten inches above the level of the garden, were coped with red Verona marble. The vasca so made received the rainfall of many paths and gave us much water. It got filled too with water-lilies and goldfish ; and with lemon trees in Venetian vases all around, with the rose borders, bamboos, and palms, the vasca plot is certainly a success.

But Venice is a thirsty place, and the supply was again insufficient. The vasca had in dry seasons to be filled with water brought in barges from the Brenta, and this was not only expensive and troublesome, but disgusted one at times when one's money had been spent on the barge-load the day before the long-desired tardy rainstorm fell.

Then I heard that artesian wells had already been sunk in Venice, and visions of running rills and splashing fountains excited our imaginations. One well, Peter told me, that had been sunk near a church and convent, was perfect in its yield and conduct, but another attempt made in a less holy place had brought itself and surroundings to fiery grief. The devil, perhaps, had toyed with its bottom and blown the water, the well itself, and the houses round to pieces.

On inquiry, I became acquainted with a well-maker from Badia Polesine, who had invented a new way of boring wells that is most ingenious, and saves some four-fifths of the expense incurred under the old system. He provides a number of iron tubes, about five inches in diameter and ten feet long. The tube to be first put in use is shod with a steel point, and the lower yard of its length is pierced with holes. This tube is planted at the spot chosen for the well, and driven into the ground as piles here are driven, by a gang of men singing a wild chaunt, much resembling that sung by the Arabs drawing water for irrigation with the sakiyas on Nile bank. The prosaic but more efficient steam-engine now replaces the men. When the first tube is up to its head in the earth a second is screwed into it and hammered down. Then another and another, and so the driving and screwing of length to length goes on till good water is reached.

Water finds its way into the tube through the holes in the lower length. During the sinking process it will rarely rise of itself to the surface, and is pumped up for testing by a pump connected with the tube for the purpose. If the main tube gets choked with mud or sand, as it often does, a small tube composed of lengths four metres long and of $1\frac{1}{2}$ inch diameter, and of similar construction to the main tube, is screwed together and passed down till it touches the impeding matter. A force-pump is then connected with the small tube, and the sand is washed up the main tube by water driven down the small one from above. The main tube cleared, the pump is disconnected, the small tube is drawn up, unscrewed length by length, and the driving of the main tube process is continued

Good water at last reached, the ordinary pump is again put to work, and for a day or two more is kept continually going to draw up the sweet water from outside through the holes in the bottom tube, and so to entice and show the way, as it were, to the spring below.

Naturally this comes charged with sand, and the sucking process is carried on until some cubic metres of solid stuff are brought to surface, leaving a hollow chamber or reservoir below of corresponding size. In this the water collects, and the flow, at first dribbling and spasmodic, becomes regular and full.

ARISTILE IPOCRATE GALIENO AVICENA ALIABTE RESIS MESVE AVER

PETRVS
DE
MONTAGNANA

CAIVS DE
PLINIVS NATVRALI

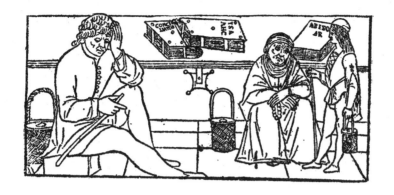

CHAPTER XI

ATCHING the well-making was very interesting. There was, of course, the element of gamble, of good water and plenty, of bad or none. The water brought up was constantly tasted, the sand was classed as coarse and good, or fine and disappointing. Once, when some thirty yards down, the tube was seen to sink at a small touch, almost with its own weight, and it was evident it was passing through water. This was tasted

and proved salt, and as in other wells made here the same thing happens it would lead one to suppose that the Venice islands are floating on a subterranean sea.

When, on the fourteenth of July last year, the Campanile of San Marco fell—that Gentiluomo, as the people called it, because it did no one any harm—I thought at first that the great shaft, with its hundred and twenty yards in height, had pierced the tired foundation and gone to the bottom of this sea, wherever that bottom might be, but a look at the debris half an hour after it fell, when the air was still thick with its dust, showed that it was the shaft itself, not the foundation, that gave way, crushed to powder by its own weight.

Below the subterranean water we came to a stratum of rock, through which the steel-pointed lower tube was driven with the greatest difficulty, blow on blow of the heavy hammer making scarcely a line-breadth's impression on resistance so great that at last the main tube was fractured with the concussion. Then the part above the

THE DIPPING WELL.

break, perhaps twenty yards in length, was drawn up. This done with very hard labour, each length as recovered was unscrewed for future use. Next, the broken lengths were fished for, but uselessly, and abandoned. So we had to begin again with some loss of gear and much of labour, planting a fresh length of tubes within a yard or so of the fractured one.

Another day we passed through peat which gave us not a little trouble. This peat would seem to be decayed and gave off gas. The gas would light with a match and often blew up without one, throwing mud and sand twenty feet into the air. The explosion choked the whole tube with debris. The force-pump was then put in action, and it often took a day or two of hard work to clear the main tube. At last at sixty metres, say two hundred feet, we arrived.

It was a most exciting moment. There was the extracted heap of sand and mud and dirt all around, and a dozen sandy or dirty men watching with triumphant looks the drops of dirty water, that all of themselves came up the tube and actually oozed out of it. This mixture, thick as water in a flood, was held up exultingly in a glass none too clean. I tasted, and with entire content declared it excellent, and so it was; the fruit of a month's hard work carrying to completion the happy useful thought of an able and honest withal old man.

Pietro had told me the blowing-up story so graphically that I had doubts of the success of an artesian well, and to remove them the well-maker put into my contract an obligation in the case of the water's failure, or insufficient yield, anywhere within ten years to make me a new well. My first well's tube was filled again and again during five years with gas explosions; as often cleared at the contractor's expense; and at the end of that time he thought it best to make a new well, and did so at a spot distant perhaps a hundred yards from the first, thanking me warmly when I voluntarily paid him half the expense.

The same demoniac symptoms, but with less virus, show themselves in this second well. To this day, eight or nine years since it was made, you may light the water, or what appears to be the water, though of course it is the gas, and see it blaze for many minutes at a time. But there have been no real explosions, and the flow of water has never ceased, though, singular to relate, the yield varies with the tide.

The rise and fall of the Venice tide is rarely more than three feet. The chamber and the vein which fills it are two hundred feet below the surface. The water that flows along that vein probably comes from the Euganean hills twenty miles away. At least they are the nearest high lands which would give the necessary fall and spring. Unless it be that the lagoon water unconsciously does the work unassisted by any fall from the hills, and by its weight and pressure on the stratum of earth which rests on the fresh water two hundred feet below, forces that water up the tube driven down to seek it. Whichever it is, the additional weight of a high tide has a marked effect on the well's yield. Is it not a rum world we live in?

So sensitive again is this spring that at the

level of the ground the discharge was some sixteen litres in the minute, say twenty-four tons in the day. Raising the mouth of the discharge pipe two feet for the purposes of distribution, reduced the yield one-third; raising it again for experiment some three feet more, and the spring became a dribble.

The well made, its water was captured for the moment in an old Venetian wellhead, or Vera di Pozzo, and led therefrom in gas-pipes underground to vaschettine made in different places for watering convenience. It was an easy and cheap mode of conveyance. But many of the pipes intended for gas would not hold water, and in a year or two required changing. It might be that their side joints, for that was the faulty part, rusted, or do gas-pipes leak on purpose to give occupation to the poor fellows who lay them with much displacement of the pavement?

To dig up, cut, unscrew, and replace the faulty tubes with new would have given much trouble, and I bethought me of merely uncovering

A VASCHETTINA.

the tubes and casing the faulty ones as they lay with Portland cement. This answered perfectly at small cost, and the doing it gave much amusement to me and my gondoliers. If you can't model busts it is more useful and not bad fun casing gas-pipes.

The water led from the vaschettine passed into the vasca grande and did me there a mischief without remedy. The day after its introduction my poor goldfish, who, in the rain-water of their tank, increased and multiplied as do Italian children of the outdoor working class (a larger reproduction could not be), came to the surface, but alas, with bellies uppermost and heads out of water seeking air instead of bread-crumbs.

They all died, poor fish, in a few days, sent off their heads perhaps by the iron in the water. The water-lilies that were thick and very floriferous did the same. And yet the water is very wholesome. My people drink it rather than cross my bridge to fill their pitchers from the aqueducts. My cows love it and thrive on it. And after passing through the vasca grande I allowed it to be carried into the neighbouring prison, whether to strengthen the prisoners in their reformation or to wash them and their work I do not know.

The Italian Government is more economic than artisans' opinions and votes allow ours to be. The prisoners here, instead of living on the rates, are taught to earn their polenta ; and hundreds of mats and carpets, of chairs and boots and shoes, are made amongst other things at our next door. More economic, certainly in the present and possibly in the future, for the *detenuti* not only pay the expense of their keep and keeping, but when, their sentence served, they are again free men, they may have acquired a habit of work and a trade that will enable them to live for instead of on their neighbours.

We are, let us say it to ourselves, justly proud of British laws and institutions ; but sometimes we may perhaps learn something from the polity of others, and surely it is better for society at large, working men included, that the man who

102

A GARDEN IN VENICE

is paying the penalty of his wrong-doing should not do so at others' cost, and should after his discharge have a chance of earning honestly enough to live on.

CHAPTER XII

WELL-MAKING was not our only earthwork pastime. We had scarcely got our garden into shape and were ready to sit under our own fig trees, to enjoy their shade and fruit, and it is so good at Venice, when we were rudely wakened from our self-congratulation by seeing huge barges discharging mud and rubble under our lagoon wall. This wall, rising on its inner side some four feet above the garden surface, and standing on its outer side, say eight or nine feet above the tide-bank, fenced us in from the lagoon.

About thirty yards from the wall is a deep canal, but the bank betwixt canal and wall was often dry at low water. The Municipio were making improvements in the city, and to give us clear comprehension of how our garden had been made, were discharging on the intervening bank the rubbish of the pulled down houses.

It was pitiful; thirty yards of mud and broken bricks and used up mortar, to be piled up between us and the lagoon. And worse. Some horrid person perhaps to lease the Sacca, as they call such reclaimed land here; to dig and plant it, and to shut us in from the open water with a screen of vines and trees, or greater horror still, of cottages.

My civil remonstrance and demonstration of

the damage that would be done me; how fatal
it was to cut us off from the view and access to
the lagoon with all its beauty and its air, was
met by the answer, made with equal civility,
that the bank was outside our property, and was
under the control of the Municipio, who would
do what they liked with their own. I had a
right to a metre's free space beyond my boundary
wall and this would be respected.

There was no redress. Private interest must
give way to the public good, and if the
Municipio thought this bank was the place to
shoot their rubbish on, we could but make the
best of it. Clearly the best was to become the
horrid person, and buy or rent the Sacca oneself.
It would take pages to tell the story of the
efforts made during fourteen years, and express
our gratitude to Prefects and Sindacos, and even
Ministers and Ambassadors, for their interest,
sympathy, and help before we arrived at the
desired proprietorship.

First we obtained a lease for three years.
The length of such leases is limited, and it is

generally prescribed that they should be put up to public auction. Think of an auction in Venice, when it was well understood that the value of the garden depended on the possession of the Sacca, and the art of Squeeze, equally well understood, is carried to perfection.

On obtaining this first lease we played the game of Brag; spent money freely on the Sacca, levelled, dug and planted it. This expenditure was made a reason for extending the lease to nine years. Then our argument was pressed at Rome and accepted, that right as it was to sacrifice the individual for the public good, no greater harm should be done to him than was necessary to carry out the public object. Therefore if the land was to be reclaimed and parted with, at least we had the prior right of purchase.

Another lease of six years was granted us, but to sell was a different matter, and difficult. For rightly the Italian law places many restrictions on the alienation of public property; but the higher authorities did us justice, and gave themselves no little trouble in so doing. And we are deeply grateful, as I think all foreigners who live in Italy may be, for the reception given them in small things and great by the Italian authorities and people.

No wonder that foreigners who have lived in Italy find it difficult to live out of it. There is the climate, the warmth, and the beauty. In no country that I know, except perhaps our own, can a reasonable man pass his time so free of restraint from law and regulation. There is no country where a foreigner will meet with such kindness and civility from the people of every class—a people, too, to whom snobbishness is unknown ; and last, if not least, Italy is the home and soil of all, save Grecian statues, that's best in art, and of these it holds the best collection.

And now, thanks, as I have said, to the Venice authorities, our garden has grown bigger by only a little less than two acres. The Sacca become a vineyard is not unproductive, and not without its charm. The once outer old sea wall, now become an inner one, has been lowered in height, so that the two plots of land may become more intimately one.

Along the inner side of this wall grow broken clumps of bays, pomegranates, and zizole, as the jujube tree, zigzaggy in its form, is phonetically named. On the outside is a border, two hundred yards in length, with an almost unbroken line of China roses, having anemones at their feet. The ground is further divided transversely with vine hedges, and has three cross paths bordered by China roses standing in a carpet of hyacinths, tulips, and wood strawberries.

The vine hedges, with their long waving and climbing shoots, green in summer, grape adorned in autumn, make a brave show in æsthetics and economy. The strips of land that divide the hedges are rich with Lucerne that, cut five times a year, gives green crops as required for the cows, or a cut of hay sweet and succulent. The view inwards shows our garden trees massed almost as a wood, from whence, its lower portion

VINE HEDGES AND IL REDENTORE.

only hidden, rise the dome and towers of the Redentore Church, that just outside calls up, let's hope, good thoughts to those that need them and lends to all the charm fine architecture adds to sylvan scenery.

The cross-paths lead to the terrace, with a summer-house thereon, at the margin of the lagoon, for refuge from the sun, and a resting-place from whence to see the glorious view.

Our frontage to the lagoon that we have been enabled to retain is also about two hundred yards in length. A broad grass terrace has been made along it, with on one side a line of round golden yews, broken by clumps of cypresses that, planted fourteen years ago, already make a goodly sight; on the other is a defending boundary wall, about three feet high on the inner side. On the outer, the wall rests on the sloping stone barrier to the tide that has been built at the margin of a deep canal used for navigation. Nothing, then, but the sails of passing boats can intercept our view, and as, winners in a hard-fought fight, we stand on the

A GARDEN IN VENICE

terrace, it is with a feeling of grateful security, as well as of Nature-lesson taught enjoyment, that we look out over the lovely lagoon to the Lido on the one side and the Euganean Hills on the other, with Chioggia in our front, hills and fishers' town each some twenty miles away.

CHAPTER XIII

OME would say the story of the garden is not complete without reference to the animal life within it. Makers of the modern garden, we are now also its head gardeners. In filling this post before we assumed it we met with many disappointments.

A GARDEN IN VENICE

The pockets of the waistcoat that held it first were found to gape very widely, and the man the waistcoat adorned, though he gave one lettuces such as I thought only grew in Covent Garden, knew nothing of flowers. So we took an Italian from the garden of a Scotch friend who had been settled in Venice for fifty years. The man was clever, but he died in little more than a year. We then had others brought from Como, and from Florence, and Lago Maggiore, but could not keep them. Probably an Italian settled in England would find some English gardeners ready to and thinking they could fairly draw profit from their master's foreign origin.

Then we imported a Scotchman, and were unlucky. The man consigned to us could not fill the place, and after five years of patience we had to send him and his wife back to Scotland with the family that had come to him.

There was then a short reign, when the throne was occupied by a lady gardener from *terra-firma*. Her master, for whom they said she had done everything, had lately died; and as both his

114

house and garden when I visited them seemed
well kept, and she had made the old man's life
easy, I hoped she might do the same for mine.

The experiment completely failed. I had to
do her work and console her that she could not
do it. Her Giudecca subjects ruled her, and after
this venture I determined to do for myself. It
was, after all, easier if one had to see that any
orders given were carried out to do so at first
hand rather than through an intermediary who
let all things drop. And then the pleasure of it
all is so much greater. The garden, ours by
rights of purchase, of laying out, and planting,
became ours all the more completely by the work
daily done within it. Not only nearly all the
trees and all the shrubs and plants were ours by
their introduction, but also by their education.
The children we brought to life we feed, fashion,
and educate in the way that they should grow.

Our aids are mostly the men who, coming to
the garden as boys, have grown up in it. Their
training has been bad, but they have lately been
more content to learn than a Venetian generally

is. Disobedience and lack of discipline are, in the lower class of the Venetians, racial qualities, and so, ingrained. On subjects on which he is ignorant he will give instruction; of his own *mestiere* knowing little, he is so proud of what he knows that he will not learn, and it takes years of training from his boyhood before you can get a man to use a Dutch hoe, or in any way to loosen the soil before he picks the weeds out of it with his hands. A broom on the paths or lawn is an insult not to be offered them, and I still get my garden roller worked by my gondoliers, who do it as a joke. It is well, therefore, to catch your gardeners early.

They have their excuse. Men who have never learnt are hard to teach. Things new are to them detestable, and the habits of their fathers, the result of years spent in saving themselves trouble, are quoted and regarded as the sum of hallowed wisdom because it allows their doing of the little that must be done in the way that is the easiest.

Then a modern garden was to them unknown;

well-swept paths, the close-cut lawns, the borders without a weed, the plants trimmed and staked, all the tidiness that goes to the keeping of an English garden, is seldom found abroad. The Italian garden in Italy means cypresses and evergreens for borders, with statues and vases of stone or marble, terraces and staircases; all very lovely things that grow or do without labour; and for flowers, pots.

These the Italian loves in hundreds, but his *poco curante* ways restrict the number of varieties. A new flower or a choice one cannot keep his continuous attention. I have had many such given me brought by ships from far distant lands. If the new-comers will accommodate themselves to the existing habit of cultivation they live. If they need special attention they die. Why should they want more or less water than the plants become their fellows in the next pots? Why should they demand a temperature more even than the varying degrees of heat and cold that have hitherto sufficed their neighbours' needs?

And really it does not so much matter to persons

like ourselves who prefer beauty to rarity. Many
rare things are also beautiful, but there are so
many that are beautiful and not rare, that where
the power of effort and the space disposable is
not unlimited, it is wise to get the best one can
with the means one has. We have then hundreds
of pot plants, survivals of the fittest, and our
entrance court where they stand in summer is
gay and much admired.

It has a door with steps running in from
the water and a land entry parallel, with steps
running in the counter sense out to our bridge
over the canal. At the sides are arranged our
pots, or what I call our Italian garden. At the
corner between the land stair and the gardener's
cottage that is clad with roses and wistaria, is a
large may tree whose blossom is brilliant red,
and a tamarisk with long feathery shoots that
hang pendent over the wall till they almost touch
the water. Next these and around them are
palms, and then jessamines and ivy-leaved geraniums trained in pyramids. Groups of arum
lilies and other high growing things with lower

118

ENTRANCE COURT , OUR ITALIAN GARDEN.

groups in front of such plants as Paris daisies, agapanthus, azaleas, Canterbury bells, geraniums in large masses of one shade, brilliant scarlet, or pink or crimson, and then dwarfer plants such as begonias, coleus, lobelia, mimulus, variegated leaved callas, and a score of others ; with a fringe in front of *Convallaria japonica,* for once acceptable, as it hides the pots, keeps them cool, and is content to grow in the earth it also hides, placed for its sustenance on the stone and brick pavement.

At the side of the Palazzina, facing the gardener's cottage, is a similar border in a curving line that marks out, whilst uniting, the groups of the plants within it; and the wall above the plants is covered with white jessamine, whilst overhead hang a couple of broad rose arches, the redundant shoots of Maréchal Niel and Reine Marie Henriette that throw themselves from the gardener's cottage across the broad-paved passage that separates it from the Palazzina.

If hard to teach, however, their gentle Italian manners make the garden men pleasant to work with, and they are not badly paid in this part of Italy. My head man, aged twenty-five, gets a hundred francs a month, and the others various sums going down to sixty. Those that like get house and fuel in the garden, others prefer to live with their families outside, and their living, as I know, is cheap, for I was once asked to act as arbitrator in a dispute they had with their caterer; the question submitted being whether they should pay him fifteen or sixteen lire the month for their whole food. So the remainder of their wages gives them a larger amount of pocket money than is probably at the disposal of any other people of their class.

This remainder is rarely badly spent; something to tobacco, something to wine, which is not dear at forty to fifty centimes a quart, and this year as low as fifteen centimes; something for clothes, also not dear in this climate, where, for say eight months in the year, a cotton shirt and trousers are sufficient dress; and a good deal to their families, for the young fellows about here, as far as I can see, spend the greater part of their wages on their fathers and mothers, till they are perhaps called to the army, when the families find them pence for their necessities and small pleasures, or till they marry, which they do as a rule very young, and their own obligations begin. The children come quick, and there is a struggle perhaps until the elder ones begin to work, when the money they earn is brought into the family budget. So taken is this for granted, that when a boy of sixteen in my service died the other day, and I expressed my very real regret to one of his family, he said, "Yes, is it not hard on his father, who will lose his salary."

Next to the gardeners come the Dachshunds, of which there were eight this spring. Alas, appreciative friends carried off four, and now there are only the grandmother, father and mother, and baby. As co-proprietors of the garden it is necessary to mention them ; indeed, what would the garden be without them ; their skins like satin, their manners of perfection, their tempers, which yield each to each without

a growl the bone they have done with ; and to
the baby, the bone only half eaten—the baby,
now of twelve months old, who owns me, who
croons for its milk, and wears a coat of plush the
colour of frosted silver.

CHAPTER XIV

HE mention of milk brings me to the cows, for our garden holds a stall and a dairy.

Milk, that education should not touch, often showed at Venice signs of over-discipline. Water is good, and flour is good, but they are out of place in the milk jug. And we, enduring what could not be helped, were sometimes constrained to accept a work of Art we did not care for in the place of a product of Nature that was good for us. One day a fine yacht, Mr. Gordon Bennett's *Namouna*, came into harbour to lay up for the summer, and I was told that she had on board a cow for sale—a splendid cow shipped from one of the ports of Switzerland. I went to see, and bought her. Namouna, as we called her, was pleased at first with the garden, but soon missed her sailors. In vain we walked her about, and added to her corn and hay and grass tempting dishes of pea halm and cabbages. She would not be comforted until we got her a companion. Some friends then who, tasting at our house Namouna's milk, preferred it to milk and water, had other friends of like tastes, and to content and supply them I bought other cows, until we have fifteen, brought down from the Italian and Austrian mountains. Two distinct breeds—one which gives much milk, one which gives much cream,

124

WINDING PATHS.

and both fair, though one, the Austrian is dark, to look at.

Before arriving at this number, the old stable having been turned to plant uses, a new one was built, partly within the walls of a pleasaunce house of the Patrician, so that no spick and span new structure might stare at us.

The fodder was at first difficult. Grass in summer cut in the orchard and brought to the stall, and hay in winter, are the staple foods of the Venetian cow, who, except to drink, rarely leaves the stable, and when she does seems in a hurry to get back to it.

To stall feed is necessary in this climate. In summer the animal would suffer from heat and flies, in winter from cold, and her feet would destroy the pastures. But I found Venice hay something like Venice milk, one was never sure of what one could buy, and to suit Namouna's fastidious taste I bought some acres at an island some three miles off, called S. Erasmo. The price paid was that of a foreigner to a native, and I was told much too high, but I had

examined well the old vineyard that had become
from neglect a meadow, and a couple of years of
kindly treatment with stall manure and Scorie
Thomas phosphates raised its yield from thirty
tons of hay to fifty-five, with grass and with
grapes in proportion.

We grow here, or the climate grows for us,
three crops of hay and an aftermath of grass.
There is a good deal of trouble in it all, but then
one must do something as long as one can do
anything, and the return for one's money would
surely please an English landlord. To visit one's
farm is the object for a run in one's launch, with
three or four water routes to choose from. It is
one of the peculiarities of Venice that to go anywhere by water there are at least three ways of
going. And another, that in the going any
slight distance you will change the tide, though
the tide does not change, and have it with you
or against you two or three times.

The lagoons discharge into the Adriatic
through several mouths that cut the Lido, that
long sea bank which for five-and-twenty miles

protects them from the sea. So in the same straight channel, if such there be, you will meet the tide against you making for the exit that is at your back, and after you have crossed the watershed, marked in one place by a tiny chapel, you will take the current with you seeking the exit that lies before you. Nor does the seeming cussedness of the current end here. Owing to the numerous islands and many canals, as one runs across the tide making for the same mouth, you may have the tide for and against you many times. In my small run of about three miles to S. Erasmo, I sometimes make this change no less than six times.

S. Erasmo is lovely. An old Venetian orchard of vines and peach, cherries, figs, pears, and apples. In spring a dream of white thorn and pink peach blossom, fenced in on two sides by the lagoon over which one looks at ancient Venice, called Torcello; the fishers' isle, Burano; and the monastery of San Francesco nel Deserto, lovely with its cypresses and isolation. In the background is the mainland, bounded by the whole range of the snowy Alps.

A GARDEN IN VENICE

We once had some hives of Ligurian bees, which, if not stingless, rarely sting. A poor fellow, poor in purse and poor in health but excellent in purpose, got them for us from I don't know where. He was a clever, single-minded and painstaking man, with a passion for fruiticulture and all things akin. The Government gave him an appointment with the duty of visiting, inspecting, and lecturing on such subjects in the Communes of the Veneto. He held some meetings, or a meeting too much, when he should have been, and knew he should have been, in bed, and died. The bees did not long survive him. They were free from vice, as was he, so that our commerce with them was as safe and innocent as was all men's with him. For a year or two they gave us honey, as did he with advice and information, but still like him they seemed to have no grip on life, and so the thrip, as I was told were called the horrid brutes that killed them, got into the hives, and though we did the best we could they died, as he did, working to the last.

A GARDEN IN VENICE

The birds in the garden are few. Birds go so well with polenta, that in spite of all one can say they are probably killed in the garden, and are certainly shot all round it. We have a few blackbirds, sometimes a cuckoo, and a nightingale yearly pays us a spring visit. But after three days he goes to join his mates on the Lido, S. Erasmo, and less inhabitated islands, where he is heard in happy numbers. It is a twofold pity, for the want of birds is our loss of pleasure and the insects' opportunity. With grubs and caterpillars we are therefore sadly pestered.

The grapes have their own devourer. A mother moth lays her eggs in the berry and worse in the stalk. The grub eats its way inside the stalk and causes rot, if let alone, to all the grapes below it.

Roses, too, have a similar enemy. A black and orange fly, the shape of and a quarter the size of a daddy-long-legs, flits in early spring from cluster to cluster of the tender rose shoots and leaves an egg in each. This egg in a day or two hatches out a small maggot, which eats its way into and down the stalk of the cluster, cutting a hole of escape when full grown and leaving its nursery dead behind it.

They tell one of cures that kill these pests, but I have found none so efficacious as handpicking.

Then we have the bobolo in too prolific numbers ; a strange snail both male and female each of itself, and yet forming a connection with another double-sexed bobolo when mating. These snails are edible, and for that reason it has been difficult to keep them under. The garden boys catch the large ones in hundreds, and do not care perhaps to destroy the breed, as they can sell them to men who put them in earthen jars to make them firm and white, and about Christmas sell them again, when they are eaten as we eat oysters.

The locust, too, visits us, and crowds of lovely white butterflies that I have learned to see killed with cruel acquiescence, in protection or in revenge of my spoiling and spoilt cauliflowers.

And mosquitoes, that have become scarce since our artesian well was made. The water from this, sulphur ferruginous, is carried, as I have said, underground to the vasca. The family mosquito, thinking the vasca a safe place in which to lay her eggs, is betrayed, for the sulpho-iron kills them, as it killed my goldfish and lilies.

Lastly, we have not the earthworm, and I at first thought Venice threw a doubt on Darwin's earthworm theory that makes them the makers of all vegetable mould. Was it the exception, perhaps, which proved the rule ? Or are there not rather in the difficulties of our cultivation some slight proofs to be found of the great man's insight.

Darwin tells how the earthworm prepares the ground in an excellent manner for the growth of all fibrous rooted plants, and seedlings of all kinds ; that their working in it is as that of the gardener who prepares fine soil for his choicest plants, and that, mixing it with their humus, they leave it in a state well fitted to retain mois-ture. They burrow, too, to a depth of five or six feet, and their burrowings allow the air to penetrate deeply, making it friable, as well as materially adding to the drainage and so helping all plants to root. Now with us newly-planted plants root with difficulty. The soil dries quickly, cakes badly, and for want of drainage is easily saturated.

The earthworm, says Darwin, drags into the soil the harder part of insects, the shells of land molluscs, and an infinite number of dead leaves and other parts of plants. This material must form a rich manure, and as their work is continuous the soil is continually renewed. With us, plants, when they have taken root, will thrive abundantly and after a year or two die out. They have exhausted that part of the soil they fed on much more quickly and entirely than they would do at home, and they die out as rapidly as they first grew. Larkspurs, for instance, sown by us one year sow themselves the next so thickly that they suffocate all other plants. In two years more the larkspur is almost extinct. So with poppies, and with antirrhinums, foxgloves, sweet-williams, and many other plants, whether sown

132

or self-sown, in a year or two their abundant vigour seems to exhaust the soil and that place knows them no more. The Iris that grow with us as people say like a weed, is no exception to the rule, and requires rather than manure that the soil they stand in should be changed, and the lilies that we so love give us only of their joy on condition that their site be changed or the fresh earth they need be brought them from another place.

So, too, Christmas roses. A single plant perhaps will thrive for years ; a plot of say twelve to twenty plants, planted together, however carefully manured, will die out in the centre of the plot after a few years' strong growth ; the outside plants in an enlarging circle still doing well. We seem to lack the worm, that kindly gardener which prepares the vegetable mould and renews it, fitting the soil for the roots of the plants, and bringing them the food they have eaten out of it ; that keeps the soil moist too with humus in dry weather, and lets the surplus water drain away in rain. One ought to import some of the

133

lobs they use or used to use in Thames punt fishing.

It is difficult to take leave of one's garden, even in writing. Though it is not an altogether selfish mistress, it is so all absorbing that even if one had the pen of a great word-painter, and could say all one would say as one would wish to say it, one might easily doddle too long over its lilies and roses, as a young man is prone to do over his lady's charms and perfections.

I will leave mine, then, advising those who have not a garden if they can to get one. Those who have, to work in it. Those who have children, to bring them up with a taste for it. I was given a garden of my own, a rake and a spade, when I could scarcely walk, and can remember still my delight when I saw the oats I had taken from the stable cornbin begin to sprout.

There is no pursuit, as has been found by big men and small, that will so readily and healthily take a man out of himself, and away from his pains and his griefs, physical or moral. If the

134

passion for games and athletics may, as we are told, be carried too far, surely that for a garden cannot be. If football and cricket may too soon be too much for us ; if bridge all day, as well as all night, is not, or may not be, entirely healthy ; gardening must be so always, and will give us occupation and delight from one's earliest days to one's end, making even the weary strive to postpone that end from the longing to see the next year's blossom.

God Almighty, Bacon tells us, planted a garden. What can we do better, who can so little do, than humbly yet lovingly strive to make another ?

135

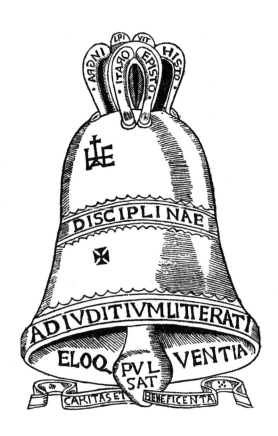

POSTFACE

Everyone in Venice – and all lovers of Venice – will have heard of the *giardino edino* or *Giardino Eden*. Very few people know, however, that Eden is the name of its first owner, let alone that one Frederic Eden has left a delightful and perceptive, if amateurish, account of what miracles an Englishman is able to perform in the city known as 'the tomb of flowers'. This charmingly illustrated book, first published in 1903 by *Country Life* and George Newnes, is not a masterpiece of literature. Mr Eden's prose is flowery and his Edwardian style whimsical. I believe, however, that it is because of this quaint style, together with the prudish Victorianized woodcuts à la *Poliphilo's Dream*, that the book ought to be reprinted.

I used to think of Giudecca as a small patch of paradise fallen on earth. For a long time I had been looking for documents about this *sestiere* of Venice – a district all the more fascinating as it seems self-possessed, away from La Serenissima. At the British Library I discovered a voluminous monograph on Giudecca, *Giudecca, Storia e Testimonianze* by Francesco Basaldella. I stared at the cover without seeing it, almost petrified in the presence of this 'tree of knowledge'. However, when I brought myself to pick up the work, it opened by chance at a strange image, a reproduction of the title page of a book. It showed the winged lion of St Mark, with a stern expression, grasping in its claws a book bearing the motto of the City of the Doges. Above it, I read the title: *A Garden in Venice*. It's author: Frederic Eden. Could this be the renowned *giardino edino*, whose name I had read on a map of Venice?

I needed to get my hands on the book right away. Fortunately, the British Library had a copy of the original in a beautiful leather-bound old-fashioned copy. From the first pages, I was captivated by the tonic health of this eccentric invalid, with that delicious gentlemanly irony which is the polite English way of asserting superiority. His description of the Feast of the Redeemer, or the building of the wells, or the purchase of one, two, three and then four cows to meet the needs of his fellow countrymen, was enough to dispel the irritation that some of his more debatable remarks aroused in me. While reading this refreshing account, I smiled at the thought that it had been published in the same year as Maurice Barrès' *La Mort de Venise*. I set about finding out more about the Edens and what had happened to their garden after their deaths.

I had learnt from Francesco Basaldella's monograph that Frederic Eden (1828–1916) was the great uncle of Anthony Eden. Unfortunately, the former Prime Minister does not breathe a word about his great uncle in his memoirs. So I turned to the one and only character mentioned in *A Garden in Venice*: Lady Radnor.

Helen, Countess of Radnor was one of the moving spirits of the English expatriate community in Venice, together with Lady Layard, Laura Ragg, Alethea Wiel, Lady Blanche Lindsay, as well as Horatio Brown, who on Monday nights played host to William Hulton, Augustus Montalba, Prince Hohenlohe, the Reverend Charles Williamson, Humpheys Johnstone and Lonsdale Ragg, to name only the winter regulars. The heart of this community, its raison d'être and its main occupation was the running of the *Ospedale Cosmopolitano*, situated just opposite the Eden's garden in Rio della Croce.

One outsider in the group was Frederick Rolfe, also known as Baron Corvo, whose biography, by Miriam Benkovitz, includes the amusing story that, being chronically short of money, he once offered his services to Frederic Eden as a poultry manager. However, Rolfe is chiefly remembered for his autobiographical *roman à clef, The Desire and Pursuit of the Whole*, which is a devastating sketch of this community whose social conscience –

according to him – was soothed by charitable works. In a biography of him, Miriam Benkovitz describes the quarrelsome relationship he had with the community in general:

> On 4 December 1909, he sent five identical letters to the members of the English Hospital's Board, Edith A. Chaffey, Lady Layard, Frederick Eden, Horatio Brown and Augustus Montalba, written in the third person and protesting against the 'unwarranted use' of Rolfe's name in the '8-month-late report' of the hosptial.

By contrast, in a long article, 'Venice When the Century was Young', in *The Cornhill Magazine* in 1936, Laura Ragg, the wife of the English chaplain in Venice, wrote this about the key figure in the colony, and Rolfe's main target:

> [Lady Layard's] position as head of our colony had been acquired without effort and was held without arrogance. She owed it in part to the fame of Sir Henry Layard, in part to her own acquired habits of authority and of responsibility for all her compatriots in a foreign land. In Venice, as formerly in Constantinople, she stood for all that was best in the British character and traditions, and the minority who resented her leadership perhaps failed to realise that the self-protective barriers raised in other cities – notably in Florence – against Anglo-American settlers were non-existent in Venice precisely because of the confidence inspired by Lady Layard.

But before turning to Enid Layard, Mrs Ragg describes at great length 'two of the [colony's] most distinguished and lovable figures . . . by then widows, continuing in London the close friendship they had enjoyed in Italy. Mme Wiel (née Alethea Lawley) . . . and

Mrs Eden (née Caroline Jekyll)'. This is a rare and valuable portrait of the Edens, their life in Venice and their garden.

[Mrs Eden] showed on the walls of her sitting-room in Seymour Street some of her late husband's graceful water-colours – views of the spacious villa and garden near Bulluno, to which she had been wont to repair during the height of summer; remaining there through early autumn. It was a spot of much natural beauty, with lovely vistas of the Dolomite Prealpi, and Mrs Eden's horticultural skill had filled the garden with scent and colour. There Mr Eden would lie for hours in a long chair beneath the trees or in the shadow of the house; and always, like the poet Lamartine, he was seen surrounded by dogs of one breed. Like the poet too he had a picturesque dignity, a grand seigneur air, an urbanity of manner which charmed all who came into his presence. In early middle life he had been crippled through exposure and a series of accidents, and he had been attracted to Venice by the ease of its waterways. His steam launch was one of the first seen on the Canals. At Belluno he had to put up with a less luxurious form of locomotion. After tea, always served in the garden, he and his wife drove out in a little victoria, usually in the direction of Socchieva, where Mme Wiel had the lease of a villa unlike any other in the neighbourhood.

Mrs Ragg goes on to praise the garden, which was undoubtedly an important local landmark:

Though Mme Wiel spoke Italian perfectly and mingled habitually and intimately with Venetians, she was less popular with them, and especially with their young people, than was Caroline Eden, whose utter lack of egotism made her the happiest woman I have ever known; that, and perhaps her success in making things grow.

She had as great a flair for horticulture as her younger sister, Miss Gertrude Jekyll, and her herbaceous borders and Belluno and on the strips of reclaimed land on the outer edge of the Giudecca were a perpetual delight and a source of occupation to her.

Save for its views over the placid waters of the lagoon 'The Garden of Eden' as it was known in the colony, had few natural advantages, but no one who saw it in the season of irises, roses, madonnas lilies will easily forget it. In warm weather about four o'clock, in the lagoon garden, tea seemed always to be on tap; and always it was made and poured by the hostess, who had a theory that no servant – least of all a Venetian – could be trusted to perform either operation.

Immediately opposite the Eden's gate, though parted from it by a narrow, bridged side-canal, was a low, and in outward aspect, rather ramshackle building, which skilful alteration had converted into the Cosmopolitan Hospital.

Since Caroline Eden was none other than Gertude Jekyll's elder sister, I consulted the biographies of Gertrude Jekyll to see what more could be gleaned about the Edens. Certain passages in Sarah Festing's biography shed important light on the couple:

In 1865, Carry was twenty-eight. . . . Carry had a wooer in Frederick Eden, commissioner of Fisheries. 'She has never liked but him,' Lady Duff Gordon marvelled, 'and at last Mr Jekyll has given in kindly.' Since Julia Hammersley's brother, Hugh, had married one of Frederick's sisters, it was the second match between the families.

Frederick had had a childhood accident and did not enjoy good health. Lady Duff Gordon had remarked earlier on her 'always sick husband', now he was 'much the same'. Before the end of the year the couple had moved to Palazzo Barbarigo in the glamorous setting of Venice's Grand Canal. No noise, no flies, no dust, Frederick remarked prosaically. Carry was, like her mother, a tireless hostess and the wonderful setting gave her an opportunity for exercising her Jekyll capacity. Soon tired of idling, her husband bought and began to cultivate a six-acre garden that formed the great work of their lives.

At Munstead House, Herbert had, with the assistance of W. J. Bean, just begun to develop a garden of Himalayan rhododendrons when the horticultural exploits of Frederick and Carry Eden in Italy were brought to public notice with a four-page tribute in *Country Life*. A little later, Frederick Eden brought out a small, beautifully illustrated leather-bound volume entirely devoted to his 'Garden of Eden'.

Frederick Eden had died in 1916 and Carry, returning to England four years later, took a house near the Brompton Oratory in Alexandra Square. Mrs Durrant remembered her as a little like Gertrude, by which she meant 'strongly artistic'. David McKenna retained the image of a frail old woman's wavery hand over a cup of tea, white hair, pendant diamond earrings and a velvet choker. In December, aged ninety-one, she too died, and Agnes remarked in an appreciation that Caroline had been 'only partially emancipated' by her marriage.

Did Gertrude Jekyll, in her own numerous works, ever mention her sister's Venetian garden, which in many respects seems to have served as her model? Yes, she did. In *Arts and Crafts Gardens* (1912), the chapter on pergolas is illustrated with two photographs which had been taken in the Edens' garden. We should bear in mind the date the garden was purchased, 1884, since, as Charles Quest-Ritson points out in *The English Garden Abroad*, 'It is very tempting to suggest that Gertrude Jekyll had a hand in the planning and planting, but she did not begin to develop her interest in gardening until several years after the Edens had completed their garden.'

Some, less sensitive to the layout of the garden, preferred to sing its best season. Such was Caroline's friend, Lady Blanche Lindsay (1844–1912), the founder, with her husband Sir Coutts Lindsay, of the celebrated rival gallery to the Royal Academy, the Grosvenor Gallery. In her book of poetry From a Venetian Balcony and other poems, she dedicated a poem to Mrs Eden entitled 'In the Time of Lilies'.

> I know a garden beautiful,
> Near by the slumbrous seas;
> Tall lilies line its dusky paths –
> 'Le roi des fleurs, le lis' –
> They spread out as a field of snow
> Betwixt the lemon-trees.
>
> A red pomegranate peeps to see
> The garden's new-wrought crown,
> And vines make roofing, lest the sun
> Should gaze too hotly down;
> Only the south wind bears away
> Sweet message to the town.
>
> All other flowers have shrunk to naught,
> And faded in despair;

Even the roses garland droop
Nor will the glory share;
This as though angels, taking hands,
Have softly floated there.

There is a wealth of literary references to the garden on which Caroline Eden liberally deployed her talents as a woman of taste. Numerous turn-of-the-century writers praised its charms. Henri de Régnier described it at length in *La Vie vénitienne* and Gabriele d'Annunzio, who knew it well, made it the location of an episode in his novel *Il Fuoco*, as did the French writer and poetess Anna de Noailles in *La Domination*. Maurice Barrès, Paul Bourget, Maurice Maeterlinck, Marcel Proust, Henry James, Rainer Maria Rilke and many others all regarded the house as an obligatory stopping place on their tour of Venice, and duly signed the visitors' book.

I have not been as lucky as Francesco Basaldella, who actually set eyes on all these signatures, but I had the pleasure of reading the dedication contained in the one copy of *A Garden in Venice* in the Bibliothèque Nationale in Paris. The book belonged to Maurice Barrès and was presented to him by Princess Edmond de Polignac (née Winnaretta Singer, daughter of the entrepreneurial inventor of the sewing machine). Her dedication reads, 'In memory of a sunny May morning in Venice' and a card, which is still kept in the book, bears these lines: 'My dear Sir, This book will remind you of our visit to the Edens' garden. Please accept it with my best wishes for the New Year to your wife, Madame Barrès and Philippe. I hope to have the pleasure of seeing you again one of these days. With my sincere best wishes. 24-12-04. (51 rue de Varenne.)'

It also pleases me to imagine that Henry James, who, as we know from his correspondence, knew the Edens, must have had their garden in mind when writing *The Aspern Papers*. The narrator, who 'must have a garden' attached to the furnished room he is looking for, has the following exchange with his future 'landlady':

> She was silent a little while after I had ceased speaking; then she began: 'If you're so fond of a garden why don't you go to terra firma, where there are so many much better than this?'
>
> 'Oh it's the combination!' I answered, smiling; and then with rather a flight of fancy: 'It's the idea of a garden in the middle of the sea.'
>
> 'This isn't the middle of the sea; you can't so much as see the water.'
>
> I stared a moment, wondering if she wished to convict me of fraud. 'Can't see the water? Why, dear madam, I can come up to the very gate in my boat.'

The passage in Anna de Noailles' novel *La Domination*, published in 1905, is also worth quoting. It is the moment when the hero, Antoine Arnault, betrays his mistress with her maidservant.

> He said to her in a low voice: 'Come tomorrow morning, at eleven o'clock, to the Eaden garden.' . . .
>
> Next day, in his gondola, on the soft green water of the canals, Antoine Arnault, tired and indolent, heads towards the beautiful secluded groves. The summer day is divine. The azure sky is like a celebration of the air, it is like a garden of blue roses, of blue dew-drops, it is like a hundred thousand wings of silver birds.

This is the passage that Marcel Proust most appreciated in his friend's novel, a work that he did not ceased to praise, even when its own author refused to have it reprinted. In a letter addressed to the Countess in 1905, he wrote: 'The most wonderful place in the book is probably this garden of Eaden (of Eden?) on the day when the azure sky is like a garden of blue roses in the air.' One can note that Proust seems better informed than the Countess about the quirkiness of English spelling. He knew that it was not necessary to turn 'Eden' into 'Eaden' for the first syllable to be pronounced with the French sound 'i'.

Did Anna de Noailles take Jean Cocteau to the garden? At any rate he wrote a poem describing a fatal event that took place on 23 September 1908, when he was nineteen. He witnessed a quarrel at the Edens between a young American, Langhorn H. Whistler, and Raymond Laurent, Cocteau's fellow student at the Lycée Condorcet, and his companion on the trip to Venice. The quarrel had fatal consequences for the young Frenchman, who ended his life with a gunshot on the steps of La Salute, just opposite a well-lit room at the Hôtel de l'Europe. After this sombre act, Cocteau wrote 'En manière d'épitaphe' (dedicated to the memory of R.L.) and 'Souvenir d'un soir d'automne au jardin Eaden' (dedicated to L.H. Whistler).

> . . . Un geste . . . un coup de revolver
> Du sang rouge à des marches blanches,
> Des gens accourus qui se penchent,
> Une gondole . . . un corps couvert . . .
> Un geste . . . un coup de revolver,
> Du sang rouge à des marches blanches . . .
>
> . . . Jardin exquisèment fatal!
> Sépulcre embroussaillé de roses,
> Si loin de la ville aux névroses,
> Si loin, si loin de l'hôpital!
> Jardin exquisèment fatal!
> Sépulcre embroussaillé de roses. . . .

Cocteau also refers to the suicide in his novel *Le Grand Ecart*:

> Jacques made fun of him about the standard suicide in Venice and wished him good night. . . . This episode had given him a distaste for the poetry of the marsh. After a walk in the Eaden garden, he still suffered from an intermittent fever that was a disagreeable reminder of his stay.

Much later, in 1958, on another trip to Venice, Jean Cocteau wrote a further poem on the garden, 'Le jardin Eaden':

> . . . C'était dans ce jardin infesté de moutiques
> A l'écart un peu de Venise
> Que nous fûmes cette surprise
> D'être deux corps vidés d'une statue antique . . .

François Mauriac was living in Venice in the autumn of 1910 with François Le Grix, and he seems to have been a frequent visitor to the Edens' garden. In 1935, in *Le Mal*, he mentions Raymond Laurent's suicide.

> It is hard, sir, it is hard to leave Venice in autumn. One does not leave Venice, sir, one wrenches oneself from it. Forgive me for saying so, but a stay in Venice is a solitary sin. . . . In front of us, sir, lay the witnesses of so many pathetic deaths: yes, over here, the steps of La Salute! One cannot even count all the young men who have chosen to die there! One of them was a friend of mine, sir. You may have read his verses, with their quain old-fashioned form. He was only seventeen and knew nothing about modern art, but he was a god. Yes, that year, I was dancing at La Fenice.

A somewhat elegaic portrait of the garden comes from the pen of Jean-Louis Vaudoyer (1883–1963). Vaudoyer, a friend of Marcel Proust and Henri de Régnier, was a critic, poet, novelist and travel writer. In *Les Délices de l'Italie*, first published in 1924, he wrote:

Every garden in Italy has one flower, or one tree, that is its living insignia, its fragrant emblem. I have already mentioned the maidenhair tree in the botanical garden at Padua and the camellias in Rome's cemetery. At Ravello shine translucent yet hardy balsams. At Paestum, blue lizards and lilac lizards scuttle among acanthus meadows. I have seen, in the public garden of Vicenza by the city gates, bold, red late-autumn sages that continue to flower even after the last chrysanthemums. Where are the most beautiful roses to be found? Without a doubt, they are in Venice, in the Eaden garden, running alongside a saltgrass path, the length of the still lagoon on the far side of Giudecca.

This garden used to belong to an English couple, who allowed people to wander through it. Its design could not have been simpler, with no contrived vistas. It could scarcely be called an architect's garden; it was almost a vegetable garden.

After a series of low, simple houses among which one might imagine a Casanova stealthily roaming about on some racy adventure in a painted gondola, you went down a narrow alley between vegetable and flower patches. Among the cabbages, a fine mango tree used to stand resplendent, like a shrine. Here and there, small pools of soft water for irrigation glinted dimly like fragments of Venetian glass flecked with ash. Also, the tombs of some favourite dog, of some cherished pet, might be found half-hidden under bushes of China roses. The long, horizontal beams of light that seem to layer the Venetian sky weighed gently over the garden, peach colours superimposed on apricot colours. Here, the sun did not set in some grand alcove couched in overblown drapery and ridiculous pelmets, as elsewhere, but on a wan, bare bed where nothing cushioned the revelation of its slow death.

This Eaden garden at dusk! The most alluring place in the world to abandon oneself to melancholy, or willingly to try to conjure up the ghosts of failed loves, lost loves. When night falls, the saltgrass path seems like a campo santo. Imagination, fed by gloomy memory and the longing heart, leads a dance of death – not the frantic, jangling dance of a medieval burial ground, but a slow, sedate dance, a procession, perhaps. You might make out a face, or half-recognize a voice. Beyond the low wall, in the still, mother-of-pearl water, here, O Ophelia, might float that white arm, a blue vein running through its precious substance. From the Zitelle, from Il Redentore, the Angelus descends like a tolling bell. Ladies in quaint old-fashioned gowns meet here. Without knowing that they are together, they leave the Eaden garden in a group to die a pretend death in a false oblivion. At the gate, Mrs Eaden's gardener offers each of these ladies a lovely bouquet of roses, picked especially for them. And, for a while, the memory of the roses will remain fragrant.

In the wake of Jean Cocteau, it appears that in the inter-war period the garden became a place of pilgrimage as well as a pick-up locale for homosexuals. This seems to be corroborated at least by what the French *auteur maudit* Renaud Camus recalls in his diary for 1989, *Fendre l'air*:

At the beginning of the 1900s, this Eden Garden, which has been occupying my thoughts, and which I went to see last month, with my mother, (but did not get in), this lush remote garden, secluded and walled in, was a 'place for encounters and adventures' (homosexual, of course), according to Jean-Pierre Joecker from *Masques*, who fortunately is mistaken in believing that it had disappeared.

Ever since 1979, most visitors have had to humbly acknowledge that, like Renaud Camus, they did not manage to get into the garden. I shall explain why, but a brief history of what happened to the garden after Caroline's death in 1928 is first necessary.

The garden was sold to Lord James Horlick, who offered it to Princess Aspasia of Greece, the mother of Alexandra of Greece. Alexandra married Peter II Karagyorgevich, the exiled King of Yugoslavia. It was while in exile herself, although, more often than not, separated from her beloved Peter, that Alexandra wrote her memoirs, *For a King's Love*. They contain several recollections of her cherished garden.

> Two years before mummie had gone to Venice and bought a most beautiful garden, nine acres of it, bounded by a canal on one side and a lagoon on the other. It had belonged to an elderly aunt of the Rt. Hon. Sir Anthony Eden (now Prime Minister of Great Britain), and so we called it the Garden of Eden, for it is a riotous wealth of all the loveliest flowers which bloom in that lush and sunny climate.

> I had not seen the French capital since Easter 1940, and I did not like to imagine the changes which war might have brought, not only to my favourite city, but also to mummie's little house in the Venice garden, from which Mussolini had driven us in 1941.

> Mummie reported from Venice that fifty A. A. gunners had occupied our tiny house during the war; three A. A. guns were still in the garden, and the whole property was in a dreadful state. But

one gondolier and his family were still there, safe and sound, and delighted to see her. 'We shall never stop working,' she wrote, 'every time they wanted wood they hacked down one of my beautiful trees, and it will take years to get the house and garden back into any sort of condition.

Though mummie had complained that much ill-treatment and neglect had damaged the nine acres of the garden, five years of peace had done much to restore it.

The cypress trees were still there, the paths still strewn with shells, and the vines still grew thickly overhead to make green cool passages. Now, in June, a tumbling bounty of fragrance and colour there were roses and jasmine, magnolias and bougainvillea. Below them grew masses of sweet peas, cool madonna and arum lilies, zinnias, begonias, lavender, rosemary, and morning-glories.

After the Second World War, Alexandra returned to Venice and lived on Giudecca until her death in 1974. Abandoned by her King, she lost her mind – the local inhabitants called her the mad woman – and the garden became the object of a curse: nobody seemed to want to have anything to do with it.

This is probably why, despite the fact that it had been declared a *monumento nazionale* after 1945, the garden was occupied by the Austrian artist Hundertwasser from 1979 until his death in February 2000. This is also when, in true Venetian style, the plot thickens, for, whenever interviewed about his domain, Hundertwasser always denied that he was the owner. 'The whole of Venice claims that I paid more than a billion for this garden, but in fact I'm not its owner,' he confided to the French writer Jean Clausel.

What is certain is that at the moment whoever tries, as I did, to get into the garden of paradise, will find their way barred by a locked gate. The garden and the villa appear to be uninhabited. On the bell one can read: 'Giardino Eden, Gruener Janura'. Gruener Janura is the company in charge of the Hundertwasser estate and they do not allow any visitors in. Had Jean Clausel been more fortunate than myself? He had had the privilege of interviewing the maestro in the garden itself. His description in *Venise chronique* is valuable testimony as to its present condition.

> On the trees, no doubt planted by the Englishman, small cherries looked like boot buttons. The painter made a point of showing me round the other cherry trees and bushy groves: 'People who don't understand anything spread it around that I am letting the garden go to waste. It's not like that at all. I love only wild plants. I am always re-planting nettles and brambles. Look how harmonious these green plants are. And the tangle of undergrowth is a veritable embroidery!'

Frédéric Vitoux, in *L'Art de vivre à Venise*, also describes the ideas of this painter-gardener: 'You don't have to tend a garden. Let nature do it instead. Practise spontaneous vegetation. Leave nature alone . . . we must enter into a dialogue with our gardens, sign a peace treaty.'

While the form of the garden has survived, Hundertwasser's conception of it was far removed from that of the Edens. It is briefly mentioned in a guide to the architecture of Venice. Under the heading 'Giudecca 137–138, Fundamenta al Rio della Croce. Giardino Eden', the entry reads: 'Belongs to the Austrian painter Hundertwasser. The garden is not open to the public and has greatly deteriorated.' So I console myself about it not being open to the public. Had I been able to get in, I would not have been able to admire any rose-laden pergolas, nor would I have been driven to share with many others my desire for a garden in Venice.

Marie-Thérèse Weal

A garden saw I ful of blosmy bowès
Up-on a river in a grenè mede,
There as ther swetnesse evermorèy now is,
With flourès whitè, blewè, yelwe, and rede,
And coldè wellè-stremès, no-thyng dede,
That swommen ful of smale fisches lighte
With fynnès rede and scalès silver-brighte.